MANHATTAN PREP

Fractions, Decimals, & Percents

GMAT Strategy Guide

This guide provides an in-depth look at the variety of GMAT questions that test your knowledge of fractions, decimals, and percents. Learn to see the connections among these part–whole relationships and practice implementing strategic shortcuts.

guide **1**

Fractions, Decimals, & Percents GMAT Strategy Guide, Sixth Edition

10-digit International Standard Book Number: 1-941234-02-X
13-digit International Standard Book Number: 978-1-941234-02-0
eISBN: 978-1-941234-23-5

Note: *GMAT, Graduate Management Admission Test, Graduate Management Admission
Council,* and *GMAC* are all registered trademarks of the Graduate Management Admission
Council, which neither sponsors nor is affiliated in any way with this product.

Layout Design: Dan McNaney and Cathy Huang
Cover Design: Dan McNaney and Frank Callaghan
Cover Photography: Alli Ugosoli

SUSTAINABLE
FORESTRY
INITIATIVE

Certified Sourcing
www.sfiprogram.org
SFI-00756

GMAT® STRATEGY GUIDES

0	GMAT Roadmap	**5**	Number Properties
1	Fractions, Decimals, & Percents	**6**	Critical Reasoning
2	Algebra	**7**	Reading Comprehension
3	Word Problems	**8**	Sentence Correction
4	Geometry	**9**	Integrated Reasoning & Essay

STRATEGY GUIDE SUPPLEMENTS

Math

GMAT Foundations of Math

GMAT Advanced Quant

Verbal

GMAT Foundations of Verbal

MANHATTAN
PREP

December 2nd, 2014

Dear Student,

Thank you for picking up a copy of *Fractions, Decimals, & Percents*. I hope this book gives you just the guidance you need to get the most out of your GMAT studies.

A great number of people were involved in the creation of the book you are holding. First and foremost is Zeke Vanderhoek, the founder of Manhattan Prep. Zeke was a lone tutor in New York City when he started the company in 2000. Now, well over a decade later, the company contributes to the successes of thousands of students around the globe every year.

Our Manhattan Prep Strategy Guides are based on the continuing experiences of our instructors and students. The overall vision of the 6th Edition GMAT guides was developed by Stacey Koprince, Whitney Garner, and Dave Mahler over the course of many months; Stacey and Dave then led the execution of that vision as the primary author and editor, respectively, of this book. Numerous other instructors made contributions large and small, but I'd like to send particular thanks to Josh Braslow, Kim Cabot, Dmitry Farber, Ron Purewal, Emily Meredith Sledge, and Ryan Starr. Dan McNaney and Cathy Huang provided design and layout expertise as Dan managed book production, while Liz Krisher made sure that all the moving pieces, both inside and outside of our company, came together at just the right time. Finally, we are indebted to all of the Manhattan Prep students who have given us feedback over the years. This book wouldn't be half of what it is without your voice.

At Manhattan Prep, we aspire to provide the best instructors and resources possible, and we hope that you will find our commitment manifest in this book. We strive to keep our books free of errors, but if you think we've goofed, please post to manhattanprep.com/GMAT/errata. If you have any questions or comments in general, please email our Student Services team at gmat@manhattanprep.com. Or give us a shout at 212-721-7400 (or 800-576-4628 in the US or Canada). I look forward to hearing from you.

Thanks again, and best of luck preparing for the GMAT!

Sincerely,

Chris Ryan
Vice President of Academics
Manhattan Prep

HOW TO ACCESS YOUR ONLINE RESOURCES

IF YOU ARE A REGISTERED MANHATTAN PREP STUDENT

and have received this book as part of your course materials, you have AUTOMATIC access to ALL of our online resources. This includes all practice exams, question banks, and online updates to this book. To access these resources, follow the instructions in the Welcome Guide provided to you at the start of your program. Do NOT follow the instructions below.

IF YOU PURCHASED THIS BOOK FROM MANHATTANPREP.COM OR AT ONE OF OUR CENTERS

1. Go to: **www.manhattanprep.com/gmat/studentcenter**
2. Log in with the username and password you chose when setting up your account.

IF YOU PURCHASED THIS BOOK AT A RETAIL LOCATION

1. Go to: **www.manhattanprep.com/gmat/access**
2. Create an account or, if you already have one, log in on this page with your username and password.
3. Follow the instructions on the screen.

Your one year of online access begins on the day that you register your book at the above URL.

You only need to register your product ONCE at the above URL. To use your online resources any time AFTER you have completed the registration process, log in to the following URL:
www.manhattanprep.com/gmat/studentcenter

Please note that online access is nontransferable. This means that only NEW and UNREGISTERED copies of the book will grant you online access. Previously used books will NOT provide any online resources.

IF YOU PURCHASED AN EBOOK VERSION OF THIS BOOK

1. Create an account with Manhattan Prep at this website:
www.manhattanprep.com/gmat/register
2. Email a copy of your purchase receipt to **gmat@manhattanprep.com** to activate your resources. Please be sure to use the same email address to create an account that you used to purchase the eBook.

For any questions, email **gmat@manhattanprep.com** or call **800-576-4628.**

Please refer to the following page for a description of the online resources that come with this book.

YOUR ONLINE RESOURCES

YOUR PURCHASE INCLUDES ONLINE ACCESS TO THE FOLLOWING:

1 FULL-LENGTH GMAT PRACTICE EXAM

The full-length GMAT practice exam included with this book is delivered online using Manhattan Prep's proprietary computer-adaptive test engine. The exam adapts to your ability level by drawing from a bank of more than 500 unique questions of varying difficulty levels written by Manhattan Prep's expert instructors, all of whom have scored in the 99th percentile on the Official GMAT. At the end of the exam you will receive a score, an analysis of your results, and the opportunity to review detailed explanations for each question.

Important Note: The GMAT exam included with the purchase of this book is the same exam that you receive upon purchasing any book in the Manhattan Prep GMAT Complete Strategy Guide Set.

5 FREE INTERACT™ LESSONS

Interact™ is a comprehensive self-study program that is fun, intuitive, and directed by you. Each interactive video lesson is taught by an expert Manhattan Prep instructor and includes dozens of individual branching points. The choices you make determine the content you see. This book comes with access to the first five lessons of GMAT Interact. Lessons are available on your computer or iPad so you can prep where you are, when you want. For more information on the full version of this program, visit **manhattanprep.com/gmat/interact**.

FRACTIONS, DECIMALS, & PERCENTS ONLINE QUESTION BANK

The Online Question Bank for Fractions, Decimals, & Percents consists of 25 extra practice questions (with detailed explanations) that test the variety of concepts and skills covered in this book. These questions provide you with extra practice beyond the problem sets contained in this book. You may use our online timer to practice your pacing by setting time limits for each question in the bank.

ONLINE UPDATES TO THE CONTENT IN THIS BOOK

The content presented in this book is updated periodically to ensure that it reflects the GMAT's most current trends. You may view all updates, including any known errors or changes, upon registering for online access.

The above resources can be found in your Student Center at manhattanprep.com/gmat/studentcenter.

TABLE *of* CONTENTS

guide **1**

Official Guide Problem Sets

As you work through this strategy guide, it is a very good idea to test your skills using official problems that appeared on the real GMAT in the past. To help you with this step of your studies, we have classified all of the problems from the three main *Official Guide* books and devised some problem sets to accompany this book.

These problem sets live in your Manhattan Prep Student Center so that they can be updated whenever the test makers update their books. When you log into your Student Center, click on the link for the *Official Guide Problem Sets*, found on your home page. Download them today!

The problem sets consist of four broad groups of questions:

1. A mid-term quiz: Take this quiz after completing **Chapter 5** of this guide.

2. A final quiz: Take this quiz after completing this entire guide.

3. A full practice set of questions: If you are taking one of our classes, this is the homework given on your syllabus, so just follow the syllabus assignments. If you are not taking one of our classes, you can do this practice set whenever you feel that you have a very solid understanding of the material taught in this guide.

4. A full reference list of all *Official Guide* problems that test the topics covered in this strategy guide: Use these problems to test yourself on specific topics or to create larger sets of mixed questions.

As you begin studying, try one problem at a time and review it thoroughly before moving on. In the middle of your studies, attempt some mixed sets of problems from a small pool of topics (the two quizzes we've devised for you are good examples of how to do this). Later in your studies, mix topics from multiple guides and include some questions that you've chosen randomly out of the *Official Guide*. This way, you'll learn to be prepared for anything!

Study Tips:

1. DO time yourself when answering questions.

2. DO cut yourself off and make a guess if a question is taking too long. You can try it again later without a time limit, but first practice the behavior you want to exhibit on the real test: let go and move on.

3. DON'T answer all of the *Official Guide* questions by topic or chapter at once. The real test will toss topics at you in random order, and half of the battle is figuring out what each new question is testing. Set yourself up to learn this when doing practice sets.

Chapter 1
of
Fractions, Decimals, & Percents

FDPs

In This Chapter...

Chapter 1
FDPs

FDPs stands for Fractions, Decimals, and Percents, the title of this book. The three forms are grouped into one book because they are different ways to represent the same number. In fact, the GMAT often mixes fractions, decimals, and percents in one problem. In order to achieve success with FDP problems, you are going to need to shift amongst the three accurately and quickly.

A **fraction** consists of a numerator and a denominator:	$\dfrac{1}{2}$
A **decimal** uses place values:	0.5
A **percent** expresses a relationship between a number and 100:	50%

$$\frac{1}{2} = 0.5 = 50\%$$

Each of these representations equals the same number but in a different form. Certain kinds of math operations are easier to do in percent or decimal form than in fraction form and vice versa. Try this problem:

> Three sisters split a sum of money between them. The first sister receives $\dfrac{1}{2}$ of the total, the second receives $\dfrac{1}{4}$ of the total, and the third receives the remaining $10. How many dollars do the three sisters split?
>
> (A) $10
> (B) $20
> (C) $30
> (D) $40
> (E) $50

To solve, you have to figure out what proportion of the money the first two sisters get, so that you know what proportion the third sister's $10 represents. It's not too difficult to add up the relatively simple fractions $\frac{1}{2}$ and $\frac{1}{4}$, but harder fractions would make the work a lot more cumbersome. In general, adding fractions is annoying because you have to find a common denominator.

On this problem, it's easier to convert to percentages. The first sister receives 50% of the money and the second receives 25%, leaving 25% for the third sister. That 25% represents $10, so 100% is $40. The correct answer is (D).

In order to do this kind of math quickly and easily, you'll need to know how to convert among fractions, decimals, and percents. Luckily, certain common conversions are used repeatedly throughout the GMAT. If you memorize these conversions, you'll get to skip the calculations. The next two sections cover these topics.

Common FDP Equivalents

Save yourself time and trouble by memorizing the following common equivalents:

Fraction	Decimal	Percent
1/1	1	100%
1/2 = 2/4 = 3/6 = 4/8 = 5/10	0.5	50%
3/2	1.5	150%

Fraction	Decimal	Percent
1/10	0.10	10%
3/10	0.3	30%
7/10	0.7	70%
9/10	0.9	90%

Fraction	Decimal	Percent
1/4 = 2/8	0.25	25%
3/4 = 6/8	0.75	75%
5/4	1.25	125%
7/4	1.75	175%

Fraction	Decimal	Percent
1/3 = 2/6	$0.\overline{3} \approx 0.333$	$\approx 33.3\%$
2/3 = 4/6	$0.\overline{6} \approx 0.666$	$\approx 66.7\%$
4/3	$1.\overline{3} \approx 1.33$	133%

Fraction	Decimal	Percent
1/8	0.125	12.5%
3/8	0.375	37.5%
5/8	0.625	62.5%
7/8	0.875	87.5%

Fraction	Decimal	Percent
1/6	$0.1\overline{6} \approx 0.167$	$\approx 16.7\%$
5/6	$0.8\overline{3} \approx 0.833$	$\approx 83.3\%$
1/9	$0.\overline{11} \approx 0.111$	$\approx 11.1\%$

Fraction	Decimal	Percent
1/100	0.01	1%
1/50	0.02	2%
1/25	0.04	4%
1/20	0.05	5%

Fraction	Decimal	Percent
1/5 = 2/10	0.2	20%
2/5 = 4/10	0.4	40%
3/5 = 6/10	0.6	60%
4/5 = 8/10	0.8	80%

MANHATTAN
PREP

Converting Among Fractions, Decimals, and Percents

The chart below summarizes various methods to convert among fractions, decimals, and percents (for any conversions that you haven't memorized!).

FROM ↓ TO →	Fraction $\frac{3}{8}$	Decimal 0.375	Percent 37.5%
Fraction $\frac{3}{8}$		Divide the numerator by the denominator: $3 \div 8 = 0.375$ Alternatively, multiply the top and bottom to get the denominator to equal 100: $\frac{3}{8} \times \frac{12.5}{12.5} = \frac{37.5}{100} = 0.375$	Divide the numerator by the denominator and move the decimal two places to the right: $3 \div 8 = 0.375 \rightarrow 37.5\%$
Decimal 0.375	Use the place value of the last digit in the decimal as the denominator, and put the decimal's digits in the numerator. Then simplify: $\frac{375}{1,000} = \frac{3}{8}$		Move the decimal point two places to the right: $0.375 \rightarrow 37.5\%$
Percent 37.5%	Use the digits of the percent for the numerator and 100 for the denominator. Then simplify: $\frac{37.5}{100} = \frac{3}{8}$	Find the percent's decimal point and move it two places to the left: $37.5\% \rightarrow 0.375$	

You'll get plenty of practice with these skills throughout this book, but if you'd like some more, see the FDPs section in the *Foundations of GMAT Math Strategy Guide*.

When to Use Which Form

As you saw in the "three sisters" problem, percentages (or decimals) are easier to add and subtract. Fractions, on the other hand, work very well with multiplication and division.

If you have already memorized the given fraction, decimal, and percent conversions, you can move among the forms quickly. If not, you may have to decide between taking the time to convert from one form to the other and working the problem using the less convenient form (e.g., dividing fractions to produce decimals or expressing those fractions with a common denominator in order to add).

Try this problem:

What is 37.5% of 240?

If you convert the percent to a decimal and multiply, you will have to do a fair bit of arithmetic:

$$
\begin{array}{r}
0.375 \\
\times\ 240 \\
\hline
0 \\
15000 \\
75000 \\
\hline
90.000
\end{array}
$$

> Alternatively, recognize that $0.375 = \dfrac{3}{8}$.
>
> $(0.375)(240) = \left(\dfrac{3}{8}\right)(\overset{30}{\cancel{240}}) = 3(30) = 90.$
>
> This is much faster!

Try something a bit harder:

A dress is marked up $16\dfrac{2}{3}$% to a final price of \$140. What is the original price of the dress?

$16\dfrac{2}{3}$% is on the memorization list; it is equal to $\dfrac{1}{6}$. Adding $\dfrac{1}{6}$ of a number to itself is the same thing as multiplying by $1 + \dfrac{1}{6} = \dfrac{7}{6}$. Call the original price x and set up an equation to solve.

$$
x + \frac{1}{6}x = 140 \qquad \frac{7}{6}x = 140 \qquad x = \left(\frac{6}{7}\right)140 = \left(\frac{6}{7}\right)\overset{20}{\cancel{140}} = 120.
$$

Therefore, the original price is \$120.

As you've seen, decimals and percents work very well with addition and subtraction: you don't have to find common denominators! For this same reason, decimals and percents are also preferred when you want to compare numbers or perform certain estimations. For example, what is $\dfrac{3}{5} - \dfrac{1}{4}$?

You can find common denominators, but both fractions are on your "conversions to memorize" list:

$$\frac{3}{5} = 60\% \qquad \frac{1}{4} = 25\%$$

$$60\% - 25\% = 35\%$$

If the answers are in fraction form, convert back:

$$35\% = \frac{35}{100} = \frac{7}{20}$$

In some cases, you may decide to stick with the given form rather than convert to another form. If you do have numbers that are easy to convert, though, then use fractions for multiplication and division and use percents or decimals for addition and subtraction, as well as for estimating or comparing numbers.

1

Introduction to Estimation

FDP conversions can sometimes help you to estimate your way to an answer.

Try this problem:

> 65% of the students at a particular school take language classes. Of those students, 40%
> have studied more than one language. If there are 300 students at the school, how many
> have studied more than one language?
>
> (A)   78
> (B)   102
> (C)   120

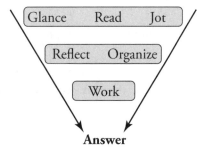

Step 1: Glance, Read, Jot: What's going on?

Glance at the problem: is it Problem Solving or Data Sufficiency? If it's Problem Solving, glance at the answers. Are they numerical or do they contain variables? Are they "easy" numbers or hard ones? Close together or far apart? If they're far apart, you can estimate!

As you read, jot down any obvious information:

$$65\% = L \quad \rightarrow \quad 40\% \text{ OF } L > 1 \text{ lang}$$
$$300 = T$$

Step 2: Reflect, Organize: What's my plan?

Okay, 300 is the starting point, but 65% is a bit annoying. You *can* figure out that number.
Do you want to take the time to do so?

If you've noticed that the answers are decently far apart, you know you can estimate. Since 65% is very close to $\frac{2}{3}$, it is a far easier number to use (especially with 300 as the starting point!).

Step 3: Work: Solve!

$$\frac{2}{3} \text{ of } 300 \text{ is } 200$$

Note that you rounded up, so your answer will be a little higher than the official number.

To calculate 40% of that number, use one of two methods:

Method 1: For multiplication, convert to fractions:

$$\left(\frac{2}{5}\right)(200) = (2)(40) = 80$$

Method 2: Find 10% of the number, then multiply by 4 to get 40%:

10% of 200 = 20, so 40% = 20 × 4 = 80

Approximately 80 students have studied more than one language. The correct answer is **(A)**.

This book will teach you how to perform proper calculations (and you do need to learn how!), but you should also keep an eye out for opportunities to estimate on GMAT problems. You'll learn multiple strategies when you get to Chapter 8, "Strategy: Estimation."

MANHATTAN
PREP

Problem Set

1. Express the following as fractions and simplify: 2.45   0.008

2. Express the following as fractions and simplify: 420%   8%

3. Express the following as decimals: $\dfrac{9}{2}$ $\dfrac{3,000}{10,000}$

4. Express the following as decimals: $1\dfrac{27}{4}$ $12\dfrac{8}{3}$

5. Express the following as percents: $\dfrac{1,000}{10}$ $\dfrac{25}{8}$

6. Express the following as percents: 80.4   0.0007

7. Order from least to greatest: $\dfrac{8}{18}$ 0.8   40%

8. 200 is 16% of what number?

9. What number is 62.5% of 192?

Solutions

1. To convert a decimal to a fraction, write it over the appropriate power of 10 and simplify:

$$2.45 = 2\frac{45}{100} = \mathbf{2\frac{9}{20}} \text{ (mixed)} = \mathbf{\frac{49}{20}} \text{ (improper)}$$

$$0.008 = \frac{8}{1,000} = \mathbf{\frac{1}{125}}$$

2. To convert a percent to a fraction, write it over a denominator of 100 and simplify:

$$420\% = \frac{420}{100} = \mathbf{\frac{21}{5}} \text{ (improper)} = \mathbf{4\frac{1}{5}} \text{ (mixed)}$$

$$8\% = \frac{8}{100} = \mathbf{\frac{2}{25}}$$

3. To convert a fraction to a decimal, divide the numerator by the denominator:

$$\frac{9}{2} = 9 \div 2 = \mathbf{4.5}$$

It often helps to simplify the fraction *before* you divide:

$$\frac{3,000}{10,000} = \frac{3}{10} = \mathbf{0.3}$$

4. To convert a mixed number to a decimal, simplify the mixed number first, if needed:

$$1\frac{27}{4} = 1 + 6\frac{3}{4} = \mathbf{7.75}$$

$$12\frac{8}{3} = 12 + 2\frac{2}{3} = 14\frac{2}{3} = \mathbf{14.\overline{6}}$$

5. To convert a fraction to a percent, rewrite the fraction with a denominator of 100:

$$\frac{1,000}{10} = \frac{10,000}{100} = \mathbf{10,000\%}$$

Or, convert the fraction to a decimal and shift the decimal point two places to the right:

$$\frac{25}{8} = 25 \div 8 = 3\frac{1}{8} = 3.125 = 312.5\%$$

6. To convert a decimal to a percent, shift the decimal point two places to the right:

$$80.4 = \mathbf{8,040\%}$$
$$0.0007 = \mathbf{0.07\%}$$

7. $40\% < \dfrac{8}{18} < 0.8$: To order from least to greatest, express all the terms in the same form:

$$\frac{8}{18} = \frac{4}{9} = 0.4444\ldots = 0.\overline{4}$$

$0.8 = 0.8$

$40\% = 0.4$

$0.4 < 0.\overline{4} < 0.8$

8. **1,250:** This is a percent vs. decimal conversion problem. If you simply recognize that $16\% =$ $0.16 = \dfrac{16}{100} = \dfrac{4}{25}$, this problem will be a lot easier: $\dfrac{4}{25} x = 200$, so $x = 200 \times \dfrac{25}{4} = 50 \times 25 = 1{,}250$. Dividing out $200 \div 0.16$ will probably take longer to complete.

9. **120:** This is a percent vs. decimal conversion problem. If you simply recognize that $62.5\% =$ $0.625 = \dfrac{5}{8}$, this problem will be a lot easier: $\dfrac{5}{8} \times 192 = \dfrac{5}{1} \times 24 = 120$. Multiplying 0.625×192 will take much longer to complete.

Chapter 2 *of*

Fractions, Decimals, & Percents

Digits & Decimals

In This Chapter...

Chapter 2
Digits & Decimals

Digits

Every number is composed of digits. There are only ten digits in our number system: 0, 1, 2, 3, 4, 5, 6, 7, 8, 9. The term digit refers to one building block of a number; it does not refer to a number itself. For example, 356 is a number composed of three digits: 3, 5, and 6.

Integers can be classified by the number of digits they contain. For example:

2, 7, and −8 are each single-digit numbers (they are each composed of one digit).
43, 63, and −14 are each double-digit numbers (composed of two digits).
500,000 and −468,024 are each six-digit numbers (composed of six digits).
789,526,622 is a nine-digit number (composed of nine digits).

Non-integers are not generally classified by the number of digits they contain, since you can always add any number of zeroes at the end, on the right side of the decimal point:

9.1 = 9.10 = 9.100

Decimals

GMAT math goes beyond an understanding of the properties of integers (which include the counting numbers, such as 1, 2, 3, their negative counterparts, such as −1, −2, −3, and the number 0). The GMAT also tests your ability to understand the numbers that fall in between the integers: decimals. For example, the decimal 6.3 falls between the integers 6 and 7:

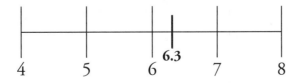

Some useful groupings of decimals include:

Group	Examples
Decimals less than −1:	−3.65, −12.01, −145.9
Decimals between −1 and 0:	−0.65, −0.8912, −0.076
Decimals between 0 and 1:	0.65, 0.8912, 0.076
Decimals greater than 1:	3.65, 12.01, 145.9

Note that an integer can be expressed as a decimal by adding the decimal point and the digit 0. For example:

$$8 = 8.0 \qquad\qquad -123 = -123.0 \qquad\qquad 400 = 400.0$$

Place Value

Every digit in a number has a particular place value depending on its location within the number. For example, in the number 452, the digit 2 is in the ones (or "units") place, the digit 5 is in the tens place, and the digit 4 is in the hundreds place. The name of each location corresponds to the value of that place. Thus:

The 2 is worth two ones, or 2 (i.e., 2×1);
The 5 is worth five tens, or 50 (i.e., 5×10); and
The 4 is worth four hundreds, or 400 (i.e., 4×100).

You can now write the number 452 as the *sum* of these products:

$$452 = 4 \times 100 + 5 \times 10 + 2 \times 1$$

2	5	6	7	8	9	1	0	2	3	.	8	3	4	7
BILLIONS	HUNDRED MILLIONS	TEN MILLIONS	MILLIONS	HUNDRED THOUSANDS	TEN THOUSANDS	THOUSANDS	HUNDREDS	TENS	UNITS OR ONES		TENTHS	HUNDREDTHS	THOUSANDTHS	TEN THOUSANDTHS

The chart to the left analyzes the place value of all the digits in the number **2,567,891,023.8347**.

Notice that all of the place values that end in "ths" are to the right of the decimal; these are all fractional values.

MANHATTAN
PREP

Analyze just the decimal portion of the number: **0.8347:**

8 is in the tenths place, giving it a value of 8 tenths, or $\dfrac{8}{10}$.

3 is in the hundredths place, giving it a value of 3 hundredths, or $\dfrac{3}{100}$.

4 is in the thousandths place, giving it a value of 4 thousandths, or $\dfrac{4}{1,000}$.

7 is in the ten-thousandths place, giving it a value of 7 ten thousandths, or $\dfrac{7}{10,000}$.

To use a concrete example, 0.8 might mean eight tenths of one dollar, which would be 80 cents. Additionally, 0.03 might mean three hundredths of one dollar, or 3 cents.

Rounding to the Nearest Place Value

The GMAT occasionally requires you to round a number to a specific place value. For example:

> What is 3.681 rounded to the nearest tenth?

First, find the digit located in the specified place value. The digit 6 is in the tenths place.

Second, look at the right-digit-neighbor (the digit immediately to the right) of the digit in question. In this case, 8 is the right-digit-neighbor of 6. If the right-digit-neighbor is 5 or greater, round the digit in question UP. Otherwise, leave the digit alone. In this case, since 8 is greater than 5, the digit in question, 6 must be rounded up to 7. Thus, 3.681 rounded to the nearest tenth equals 3.7. Note that all the digits to the right of the right-digit-neighbor are irrelevant when rounding.

Rounding appears on the GMAT in the form of questions such as this:

> If x is the decimal 8.1d5, with d as an unknown digit, and x rounded to the nearest tenth is equal to 8.1, which digits could not be the value of d?

In order for x to be 8.1 when rounded to the nearest tenth, the right-digit-neighbor, d, must be less than 5. Therefore, d cannot be 5, 6, 7, 8 or 9.

Powers of 10: Shifting the Decimal

What are the patterns in the below table?

In words	thousands	hundreds	tens	ones	tenths	hundredths	thousandths
In numbers	1,000	100	10	1	0.1	0.01	0.001
In powers of ten	10^3	10^2	10^1	10^0	10^{-1}	10^{-2}	10^{-3}

The place values continually decrease from left to right by powers of 10. Understanding this can help you understand the following shortcuts for multiplication and division.

When you multiply any number by a positive power of 10, move the decimal to the right the specified number of places. This makes positive numbers larger:

$3.9742 \times 10^3 = 3,974.2$ Move the decimal to the right 3 spaces.

$89.507 \times 10 = 895.07$ Move the decimal to the right 1 space.

When you divide any number by a positive power of 10, move the decimal to the left the specified number of places. This makes positive numbers smaller:

$4,169.2 \div 10^2 = 41.692$ Move the decimal to the left 2 spaces.

$89.507 \div 10 = 8.9507$ Move the decimal to the left 1 space.

Sometimes, you will need to add zeroes in order to shift a decimal:

$2.57 \times 10^6 = 2,570,000$ Add 4 zeroes at the end.

$14.29 \div 10^5 = 0.0001429$ Add 3 zeroes at the beginning.

Finally, note that negative powers of 10 reverse the regular process. Multiplication makes the number smaller and division makes the number larger:

$6,782.01 \times 10^{-3} = 6.78201$ $53.0447 \div 10^{-2} = 5,304.47$

You can think about these processes as trading decimal places for powers of 10.

For instance, all of the following numbers equal 110,700:

110.7	$\times$	10^3
11.07	$\times$	10^4
1.107	$\times$	10^5
0.1107	$\times$	10^6
0.01107	$\times$	10^7

The number in the first column gets smaller by a factor of 10 as you move the decimal one place to the left, but the number in the second column gets bigger by a factor of 10 to compensate, so the overall number still equals 110,700.

MANHATTAN
PREP

Decimal Operations

Addition & Subtraction

To add or subtract decimals, first line up the decimal points. Then add zeroes to make the right sides of the decimals the same length:

4.319 + 221.8

Line up the
decimal points
and add zeroes.

$$
\begin{array}{r}
4.319 \\
+\ 221.800 \\
\hline
226.119
\end{array}
$$

10 − 0.063

Line up the
decimal points
and add zeroes.

$$
\begin{array}{r}
10.000 \\
-\ 0.063 \\
\hline
9.937
\end{array}
$$

> **Addition and subtraction:** Line up the decimal points!

Multiplication

To multiply decimals, ignore the decimal point until the end. Just multiply the numbers as you would if they were whole numbers. Then count the total number of digits to the right of the decimal point in the starting numbers. The product should have the same number of digits to the right of the decimal point.

0.02 × 1.4

Count the digits to the
right of the decimal:

3

Multiply
normally:

$$
\begin{array}{r}
14 \\
\times\ 2 \\
\hline
28
\end{array}
$$

Move the decimal
3 places to the left:

28 → 0.028

If the product ends with 0, that 0 still counts as a place value. For example: 0.8 × 0.5 = 0.40, since 8 × 5 = 40.

> **Multiplication:** Count all the digits to the right of the decimal point—then multiply normally, ignoring the decimals. Finally, put the same number of decimal places in the product.

If you are multiplying a very large number and a very small number, the following trick works to simplify the calculation: move the decimals the same number of places, but *in the opposite direction*.

0.0003 × 40,000 = ?

Move the decimal point *right* four places on the 0.0003 ⟶ 3
Move the decimal point *left* four places on the 40,000 ⟶ 4

0.0003 × 40,000 = 3 × 4 = 12

This technique works because you are multiplying and then dividing by the same power of 10. In other words, you are trading decimal places in one number for decimal places in another number. This is just like trading decimal places for powers of 10, as you saw earlier.

Division

If there is a decimal point in the dividend (the number under the division sign) only, you can simply bring the decimal point straight up to the answer and divide normally:

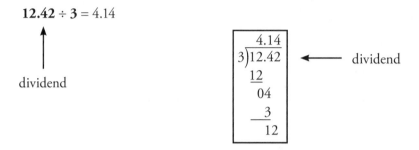

However, if there is a decimal point in the divisor (the outer number), shift the decimal point in both the divisor and the dividend to make the *divisor* a whole number. Then, bring the decimal point up and divide:

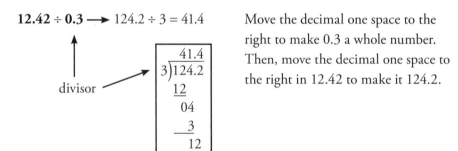

Move the decimal one space to the right to make 0.3 a whole number. Then, move the decimal one space to the right in 12.42 to make it 124.2.

> **Division:** Divide by whole numbers! Move the decimal in both numbers so that the divisor is a whole number.

You can always simplify division problems that involve decimals by shifting the decimal point *in the same direction* in both the divisor and the dividend, even when the division problem is expressed as a fraction:

$$\frac{0.0045}{0.09} = \frac{45}{900}$$

Move the decimal 4 spaces to the right to make both the numerator and the denominator whole numbers.

Note that this is essentially the same process as simplifying a fraction. You multiply the numerator and denominator of the fraction by a power of 10—in this case, 10^4, or 10,000.

Keep track of how you move the decimal point! To simplify multiplication, you can move decimals in *opposite* directions. But to simplify division, move decimals in the *same* direction.

Problem Set

Solve each problem, applying the concepts and rules you learned in this section.

1. In the decimal, 2.4d7, d represents a digit from 0 to 9. If the value of the decimal rounded to the nearest tenth is less than 2.5, what are the possible values of d?

2. Simplify: $\dfrac{0.00081}{0.09}$

3. Which integer values of b would give the number $2002 \div 10^{-b}$ a value between 1 and 100?

4. Simplify: $(4 \times 10^{-2}) - (2.5 \times 10^{-3})$

Save the below problem set for review, either after you finish this book or after you finish all of the Quant books that you plan to study.

5. If k is an integer, and if 0.02468×10^{k} is greater than 10,000, what is the least possible value of k?

6. What is $4{,}563{,}021 \div 10^{5}$, rounded to the nearest whole number?

7. Which integer values of j would give the number $-37{,}129 \times 10^{j}$ a value between -100 and -1?

Solutions

1. **{0, 1, 2, 3, 4}:** If d is 5 or greater, the decimal rounded to the nearest tenth will be 2.5.

2. **0.009:** Shift the decimal point 2 spaces to eliminate the decimal point in the denominator:

$$\frac{0.00081}{0.09} = \frac{0.081}{9}$$

Now divide. First, drop the 3 decimal places: $81 \div 9 = 9$. Then put the 3 decimal places back: 0.009.

3. **{–2, –3}:** In order to give 2002 a value between 1 and 100, you must shift the decimal point to change the number to 2.002 or 20.02. This requires a shift of either two or three places to the left. Remember that while multiplication shifts the decimal point to the right, division shifts it to the left. To shift the decimal point 2 places to the left, you would divide by 10^2. To shift it 3 places to the left, you would divide by 10^3. Therefore, the exponent $–b$ is equal to {2, 3}, and b is equal to {–2, –3}.

4. **0.0375:** First, rewrite the numbers in standard notation by shifting the decimal point. Then, add zeroes, line up the decimal points, and subtract:

$$\begin{array}{r} 0.0400 \\ -\ 0.0025 \\ \hline 0.0375 \end{array}$$

5. **6:** Multiplying 0.02468 by a positive power of 10 will shift the decimal point to the right. Simply shift the decimal point to the right until the result is greater than 10,000. Keep track of how many times you shift the decimal point. Shifting the decimal point 5 times results in 2,468. This is still less than 10,000. Shifting one more place yields 24,680, which is greater than 10,000.

6. **46:** To divide by a positive power of 10, shift the decimal point to the left. This yields 45.63021. To round to the nearest whole number, look at the tenths place. The digit in the tenths place, 6, is more than 5. Therefore, the number is closest to 46.

7. **{–3, –4}:** In order to give –37,129 a value between –100 and –1, you must shift the decimal point to change the number to –37.129 or –3.7129. This requires a shift of either 3 or 4 places to the left. Remember that multiplication by a positive power of 10 shifts the decimal point to the right. To shift the decimal point 3 places to the left, you would multiply by 10^{-3}. To shift it 4 places to the left, you would multiply by 10^{-4}. Therefore, the exponent j is equal to {–3, –4}.

Chapter 3
of
Fractions, Decimals, & Percents

Strategy: Test Cases

In This Chapter...

Chapter 3
Strategy: Test Cases

Certain problems allow for multiple possible scenarios, or cases. When you **test cases**, you try different numbers in a problem to see whether you have the same outcome or different outcomes.

The strategy plays out a bit differently for Data Sufficiency (DS) compared to Problem Solving. This chapter will focus on DS problems; if you have not yet studied DS, please see Appendix A of this guide. For a full treatment of Problem Solving, see the Strategy: Test Cases chapter in the *Number Properties GMAT Strategy Guide*.

Try this problem, using any solution method you like:

> If *x* is a positive integer, what is the units digit of *x*?
>
> (1) The units digit of $\dfrac{x}{10}$ is 4.
>
> (2) The tens digit of 10*x* is 5.

How to Test Cases

Here's how to test cases to solve the above problem:

Step 1: What possible cases are allowed?

The problem doesn't seem to give you much: the number *x* is a positive integer. You do know one more thing, though: the units digit can consist of only a single digit. By definition, then, the units digit of *x* has to be one of the numbers 0, 1, 2, 3, 4, 5, 6, 7, 8, or 9. (Some problems could limit your options further by, for example, indicating that *x* is even.)

Step 2: Choose numbers that work for the statement.

Before you dive into the work, remember this crucial rule:

When choosing numbers to test cases, ONLY choose numbers that are allowed by that statement.

If you inadvertently choose numbers that make the statement false, discard that case and try again.

Step 3: Try to prove the statement *insufficient*.

Here's how:

    (1) The units digit of $\frac{x}{10}$ is 4.

What numbers would make this statement true?

Case 1: $x = 45$:

Statement true? (units digit $\frac{x}{10}$ = 4)	Units digit of x?
$\frac{45}{10} = 4.5$ ✓	5

First, ensure that the value you've chosen to test does make the statement true. In this case, the units digit of $\frac{45}{10}$ is 4, so $x = 45$ is a valid number to test. If you had chosen, say, 54, then the units digit of $\frac{54}{10}$ would be 5, not 4, so you would discard that case.

Second, answer the question asked. If $x = 45$, then the units digit of x is 5.

Next, ask yourself: Is there another possible case that would give you a *different* outcome?

Case 2: $x = 46$:

Statement true? (units digit $\frac{x}{10}$ = 4)	Units digit of x?
$\frac{46}{10} = 4.6$ ✓	6

Because there are at least two possible values for the units digit, this statement is not sufficient; cross off answers (A) and (D) on your answer grid.

~~AD~~

BCE

MANHATTAN
PREP

Try statement (2) next:

(2) The tens digit of $10x$ is 5.

Case 1: $x = 45$:

Statement true? (tens digit $10x = 5$)	Units digit of x?
$10x = 450$ ✓	5

Is there another possible case that would give you a different outcome?

Case 2: $x = 46$:

Statement true? (tens digit $10x = 5$)	Units digit of x?
$10x = 460$ ✗	

Careful! The tens digit of 460 is *not* 5. You have to pick a value that makes statement (2) true. Discard this case. (Literally cross it off on your scrap paper.)

Case 3: $x = 65$.

Statement true? (tens digit $10x = 5$)	Units digit of x?
$10x = 650$ ✓	5

The units digit of x is 5, once again. Hmm.

It turns out that, no matter how many cases you try for statement (2), the units digit of x will always be 5. Why?

When you multiply x by 10, what used to be the units digit becomes the tens digit. If you know that the tens digit of the new number is 5, then the units digit of the original number also has to be 5. This statement is sufficient.

The correct answer is **(B)**.

When you test cases in Data Sufficiency, your ultimate goal is to try to prove the statement insufficient, if you can. The first case you try will give you one outcome. For the next case, think about what numbers would be likely to give a *different* outcome.

As soon as you do find two different outcomes, as in statement (1) above, you know the statement is not sufficient, and you can cross off some answer choices and move on.

If you have tried several times to prove the statement insufficient but you keep getting the same outcome, then that statement is probably sufficient. You may be able to prove to yourself why you will always get the same outcome, as in statement (2) above. However, if you can't do that in a reasonable amount of time, you may need to assume you've done enough and move on. When it's time to review your work, take the time to try to understand why the result was always the same.

Try another problem:

If $a = 2.4d7$, and d represents a digit from 0 to 9, is d greater than 4?

(1) If a were rounded to the nearest hundredth, the new number would be greater than a.

(2) If a were rounded to the nearest tenth, the new number would be greater than a.

Step 1: What possible cases are allowed?

The variable d represents a digit, so it could be any number from 0 to 9. There are no additional constraints to begin with, but you do have one more thing to consider.

The question is different this time: it doesn't ask for the value of d, it just asks whether d is greater than 4. When you have a yes/no question, make sure you understand (before you begin!) what would be sufficient and what would not be sufficient.

In this case, if you know that d is 4 or less, then the answer to the question is no and the statement is sufficient. If you know that d is greater than 4, then the answer to the question is yes and the statement is sufficient. This is true even if you do not know exactly what d is.

If the possible values cross the barrier of 4 (e.g., d could be 4 or 5), then the statement is not sufficient.

Step 2: Choose numbers that work for the statement.

The statements are pretty complicated; it would be easy to make a mistake with this. Remind yourself to separate your evaluation into two parts. First, have you chosen numbers that do make this statement true? Second, is the answer to the question yes or no based on this one case?

Step 3: Try to prove the statement *insufficient.*

(1) If a were rounded to the nearest hundredth, the new number would be greater than a.

The hundredth digit of $a = 2.4d7$ is the variable d. If $d = 5$, then $a = 2.457$. Rounding to the nearest hundredth produces 2.46, which is indeed greater than 2.457. It's acceptable, then, to choose $d = 5$.

Next, is d greater than 4? Yes, in this case, it is.

Can you think of another case that would give the opposite answer, a no?

Try $d = 3$. In this case $a = 2.437$. Rounding to the nearest hundredth produces 2.44, which is indeed greater than 2.437. It's acceptable, then, to choose $d = 3$, and in this case, the answer to the question is no, d is not greater than 4.

MANHATTAN
PREP

Because you're getting Sometimes Yes, Sometimes No, this statement is not sufficient to answer the question. Cross off answers (A) and (D). Now look at statement (2):

(2) If *a* were rounded to the nearest tenth, the new number would be greater than *a*.

The tenths digit of $a = 2.4d7$ is 4. Find a value of *d* that will make this statement true. If $d = 9$, then $a = 2.497$. Rounding to the nearest tenth produces 2.5, which is greater than 2.497, so 9 is an acceptable number to choose.

In this case, yes, *d* is greater than 4.

Try to find another acceptable number that will give you the opposite answer, no. If $d = 3$, then $a = 2.437$, and the rounded number is 2.4. Wait a second! 2.4 is not larger than 2.437. You can't pick $d = 3$.

What about 4? Then $a = 2.447$, which still rounds down to 2.4. In fact, any number below 5 will cause *a* to round down to 2.4, which contradicts the statement. The only acceptable values for *d* are 5, 6, 7, 8, and 9.

Is *d* greater than 4? Yes, always, so statement (2) is sufficient. The correct answer is (B).

In sum, when you are asked to test cases, follow three main steps:

Step 1: What possible cases are allowed?

Before you start solving, make sure you know what restrictions have been placed on the basic problem in the question stem. You may be told to use the 10 digits, or that the particular number is positive, or odd, and so on. Follow these restrictions when choosing numbers to try later in your work.

Step 2: Choose numbers that work for the statement.

Pause for a moment to remind yourself that you are only allowed to choose numbers for each statement that make that particular statement true. With enough practice, this will begin to become second nature. If you answer a Testing Cases problem incorrectly but aren't sure why, see whether you accidentally tested cases that weren't allowed because they didn't make the statement true.

Step 3: Try to prove the statement *insufficient*.

Value

>   Sufficient: single numerical answer
>   Not Sufficient: two or more possible answers

Yes/No

>   Sufficient: Always Yes *or* Always No
>   Not Sufficient: Maybe or Sometimes Yes, Sometimes No

When to Test Cases

You can test cases whenever a Data Sufficiency problem allows multiple possible starting points. In that case, try some of the different possibilities allowed in order to see whether different scenarios, or cases, result in different answers or in the same answer.

All problems will have one thing in common: your initial starting point is every possible number on the number line. The problem then may give you certain restrictions that narrow the possible values. As you saw above, the digit constraint (0, 1, 2, 3, 4, 5, 6, 7, 8, or 9) is one possible restriction.

Other common restrictions include classes of numbers that react differently to certain mathematical operations. For instance, positive and negative numbers have different properties, as do odds and evens. Integers and fractions can also have different properties, particularly proper fractions (those between 0 and 1). You'll learn more about proper fractions in the next chapter of this book.

How to Get Better at Testing Cases

First, try the problems associated with this chapter in your online *Official Guide* problem sets. Work each problem using the three-step process for testing cases. If you mess up any part of the process, try the problem again, making sure to write out all of your work.

Afterwards, review the problem. In particular, when a statement is sufficient because it produces the same answer in each case, see whether you can articulate the reason (as the solutions to the earlier problems did). Could you explain to a fellow student who is confused? If so, then you are starting to learn both the process by which you test cases and the underlying principles that these kinds of problems test.

If not, then look up the solution in GMAT Navigator™, consult the Manhattan Prep forums, or ask an instructor or fellow student for help.

Chapter 4

of

Fractions, Decimals, & Percents

Fractions

In This Chapter...

Chapter 4
Fractions

Decimals are one way of expressing the numbers that fall in between the integers. Another way of expressing these numbers is fractions.

For example, the fraction $\dfrac{13}{2}$, which equals 6.5, falls between the integers 6 and 7:

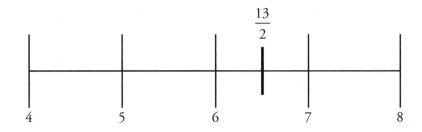

Proper fractions are those that fall between 0 and 1. In proper fractions, the numerator is always smaller than the denominator. For example:

$$\frac{1}{4}, \frac{1}{2}, \frac{2}{3}, \frac{7}{10}$$

Improper fractions are those that are greater than or equal to 1. In improper fractions, the numerator is greater than or equal to the denominator. For example:

$$\frac{5}{4}, \frac{13}{2}, \frac{11}{3}, \frac{101}{10}$$

Improper fractions can be rewritten as **mixed numbers**. A mixed number is an integer and a proper fraction. For example:

$$\frac{5}{4}=1\frac{1}{4} \qquad \frac{13}{2}=6\frac{1}{2} \qquad \frac{11}{3}=3\frac{2}{3} \qquad \frac{101}{10}=10\frac{1}{10}$$

Although the preceding examples use positive fractions, note that fractions and mixed numbers can be negative as well.

Numerator and Denominator Rules

Certain key rules govern the relationship between the **numerator** (the top number) and the **denominator** (the bottom number) of proper fractions. These rules apply only to positive fractions.

If you increase the numerator of a fraction, while holding the denominator constant, the fraction increases in value:

$$\frac{1}{8}<\frac{2}{8}<\frac{3}{8}<\frac{4}{8}<\frac{5}{8}<\frac{6}{8}<\frac{7}{8}<\frac{8}{8}<\frac{9}{8}<\frac{10}{8}<\dots$$

If you increase the denominator of a fraction, while holding the numerator constant, the fraction decreases in value as it approaches 0:

$$\frac{3}{2}>\frac{3}{3}>\frac{3}{4}>\frac{3}{5}>\frac{3}{6}\dots>\frac{3}{1,000}\dots\to 0$$

Adding the same number to *both* the numerator and the denominator brings the fraction *closer* to 1, regardless of the fraction's value.

If the fraction is originally smaller than 1, the fraction *increases* in value as it approaches 1:

$$\frac{1}{2}<\frac{1+1}{2+1}=\frac{2}{3}<\frac{2+9}{3+9}=\frac{11}{12}<\frac{11+1,000}{12+1,000}=\frac{1,011}{1,012}$$

Thus: $\dfrac{1}{2}<\dfrac{2}{3}<\dfrac{11}{12}<\dfrac{1,011}{1,012}\dots\to 1$

Conversely, if the fraction is originally larger than 1, the fraction *decreases* in value as it approaches 1:

$$\frac{3}{2}>\frac{3+1}{2+1}=\frac{4}{3}>\frac{4+9}{3+9}=\frac{13}{12}>\frac{13+1,000}{12+1,000}=\frac{1,013}{1,012}$$

Thus: $\dfrac{3}{2}>\dfrac{4}{3}>\dfrac{13}{12}>\dfrac{1,013}{1,012}\dots\to 1$

Simplifying Fractions

Simplifying is a way to express a fraction in its lowest terms. Fractional answers on the GMAT will always be presented in fully simplified form. The process of simplifying is governed by one simple rule: multiplying or dividing both the numerator and the denominator by the same number does not change the value of the fraction:

$$\frac{24}{30} = \frac{24 \div 6}{30 \div 6} = \frac{4}{5} \qquad\qquad \frac{4}{5} = \frac{4(3)}{5(3)} = \frac{12}{15} = \frac{12(2)}{15(2)} = \frac{24}{30}$$

Simplifying a fraction means dividing both the numerator and the denominator by a common factor until no common factors remain:

$$\frac{40}{30} = \frac{40 \div 5}{30 \div 5} = \frac{8}{6} = \frac{8 \div 2}{6 \div 2} = \frac{4}{3} \qquad \text{or in one step:} \qquad \frac{40}{30} = \frac{40 \div 10}{30 \div 10} = \frac{4}{3}$$

Converting Mixed Numbers to Improper Fractions

In order to convert a mixed number into an improper fraction (something you need to do in order to multiply or divide mixed numbers), use the following procedure:

$$2\frac{1}{4}$$ Multiply the whole number (2) by the denominator (4) and add the numerator (1).

$$2 \times 4 + 1 = 9$$ Now place the number 9 over the original denominator (4): $\frac{9}{4}$.

Alternatively, since $2\frac{1}{4} = 2 + \frac{1}{4}$, just split the mixed fraction into its two parts and rewrite the whole number using a common denominator:

$$2\frac{1}{4} = 2 + \frac{1}{4} = \frac{8}{4} + \frac{1}{4} = \frac{9}{4}$$

Simplify Before You Multiply

When multiplying fractions, you could first multiply the numerators together, then multiply the denominators together, and finally simplify the resulting product. For example:

$$\frac{8}{15} \times \frac{35}{72} = \frac{8(35)}{15(72)} = \frac{280}{1,080} = \frac{28}{108} = \frac{7}{27}$$

This is pretty painful without a calculator, though. Instead, simplify the fractions before you multiply: cancel similar terms from the top and bottom of the fractions.

Notice that the **8** in the numerator and the **72** in the denominator both have 8 as a factor. Thus, they can be simplified from $\frac{8}{72}$ to $\frac{1}{9}$. It doesn't matter that the numbers appear in two different fractions. When multiplying fractions together, you can treat all of the numerators as one group, and all of the denominators as another. You can cancel anything in the top group with anything in the bottom.

Notice also that **35** in the numerator and **15** in the denominator both have 5 as a factor. Thus, they can be simplified from $\frac{35}{15}$ to $\frac{7}{3}$.

Now the multiplication will be easier and no further simplification will be necessary:

$$\frac{{}^1\cancel{8}}{{}_3\cancel{15}} \times \frac{\cancel{35}\,^7}{\cancel{72}\,_9} = \frac{1(7)}{3(9)} = \frac{7}{27}$$

Always try to cancel factors before multiplying fractions!

In order to multiply mixed numbers, first convert each mixed number into an improper fraction:

$$2\frac{1}{3} \times 6\frac{3}{5} = \frac{7}{3} \times \frac{33}{5}$$

Then simplify before you multiply:

$$\frac{7}{{}_1\cancel{3}} \times \frac{\cancel{33}\,^{11}}{5} = \frac{7(11)}{1(5)} = \frac{77}{5}$$

Add and Subtract: Use a Common Denominator

In order to add or subtract fractions, follow these steps:

1. Find a common denominator.

2. Change each fraction so that it is expressed using this common denominator.

3. Add up the numerators only.

Here's an example:

$$\frac{3}{8} + \frac{7}{12}$$

$$\frac{9}{24} + \frac{14}{24}$$ A common denominator is 24. Thus, $\frac{3}{8} = \frac{9}{24}$ and $\frac{7}{12} = \frac{14}{24}$.

$$\frac{9}{24} + \frac{14}{24} = \frac{23}{24}$$ Finally, add the numerators to find the answer.

In this example, you have to simplify the fraction at the end:

$$\frac{11}{15} - \frac{7}{30}$$

$$\frac{22}{30} - \frac{7}{30}$$ A common denominator is 30. $\frac{11}{15} = \frac{22}{30}$ and $\frac{7}{30}$ stays the same.

$$\frac{22}{30} - \frac{7}{30} = \frac{15}{30}$$ Subtract the numerators.

$$\frac{15}{30} = \frac{1}{2}$$ Simplify $\frac{15}{30}$ to find the answer: $\frac{1}{2}$.

In order to add or subtract mixed numbers, first convert to improper fractions and then solve as shown above.

Dividing Fractions: Use the Reciprocal

In order to divide fractions, use the reciprocal. You can think of the reciprocal as the fraction flipped upside down:

The reciprocal of $\frac{3}{4}$ is $\frac{4}{3}$.   The reciprocal of $\frac{2}{9}$ is $\frac{9}{2}$.

What is the reciprocal of an integer? Think of an integer as a fraction with a denominator of 1. Thus, the integer 5 is really just $\frac{5}{1}$. To find the reciprocal, just flip it:

The reciprocal of **5,** or $\frac{5}{1}$, is $\frac{1}{5}$.   The reciprocal of **8** is $\frac{1}{8}$.

In order to divide fractions, follow these steps:

    1. Change the divisor into its reciprocal (the divisor is the second number).
    2. Multiply the fractions.

For example:

$$\frac{1}{2} \div \frac{3}{4}$$

First, change the divisor $\frac{3}{4}$ into its reciprocal $\frac{4}{3}$.

$$\frac{1}{\underset{1}{2}} \times \frac{\overset{2}{4}}{3} = \frac{2}{3}$$

Then simplify if needed and multiply to find the answer.

Split Up Double-Decker Fractions

The division of fractions can be shown by using the division sign, or by putting the fractions themselves into a fraction. Consider one of the previous examples:

$\frac{1}{2} \div \frac{3}{4}$ can also be written as a "double-decker" fraction this way:

$$\dfrac{\dfrac{1}{2}}{\dfrac{3}{4}}$$

You can rewrite this as the top fraction divided by the bottom fraction, and solve normally by using the reciprocal of the bottom fraction and then multiplying:

$$\dfrac{\dfrac{1}{2}}{\dfrac{3}{4}} = \frac{1}{2} \div \frac{3}{4} = \frac{1}{2} \times \frac{4}{3} = \frac{2}{3}$$

In addition, you can often simplify quickly by multiplying both top and bottom by a common denominator:

$$\dfrac{\dfrac{1}{2}}{\dfrac{3}{4}} = \dfrac{\dfrac{1}{2} \times 4}{\dfrac{3}{4} \times 4} = \frac{2}{3}$$

Comparing Fractions: Cross-Multiply

Which fraction is greater, $\dfrac{7}{9}$ or $\dfrac{4}{5}$?

The traditional method of comparing fractions involves finding a common denominator and comparing the two fractions. The common denominator of 9 and 5 is 45.

Thus, $\dfrac{7}{9} = \dfrac{35}{45}$ and $\dfrac{4}{5} = \dfrac{36}{45}$. In this case, $\dfrac{4}{5}$ is slightly greater than $\dfrac{7}{9}$.

However, there is a shortcut to comparing fractions: cross-multiplication. This is a process that involves multiplying the numerator of one fraction by the denominator of the other fraction, and vice versa:

$(7 \times 5) = 35$ $(4 \times 9) = 36$

$\dfrac{7}{9}$ ⤢ $\dfrac{4}{5}$ Set up the fractions next to each other.

Cross-multiply the fractions and put each answer by the corresponding numerator (*not* the denominator!)

$\dfrac{7}{9}$ $<$ $\dfrac{4}{5}$ Since 35 is less than 36, the first fraction must be less than the second one.

Essentially, you have done the same thing as before—you just didn't bother to write the common denominator. This process can save you a lot of time when comparing fractions on the GMAT.

Complex Fractions: Don't Split the Denominator

A complex fraction is a fraction in which there is a sum or a difference in the numerator or the denominator. Three examples of complex fractions are:

(a) $\dfrac{15+10}{5}$ (b) $\dfrac{5}{15+10}$ (c) $\dfrac{15+10}{5+2}$

In example (a), the numerator is expressed as a sum.
In example (b), the denominator is expressed as a sum.
In example (c), both the numerator and the denominator are expressed as sums.

When simplifying fractions that incorporate sums or differences, remember this rule: You may split up the terms of the numerator, but you may *never* split the terms of the denominator.

For example, the terms in example (a) may be split into two fractions:

$$\frac{15+10}{5} = \frac{15}{5} + \frac{10}{5} = 3 + 2 = 5$$

But the terms in example (b) may not be split:

$$\frac{5}{15+10} \neq \frac{5}{15} + \frac{5}{10} \quad \textbf{NO!}$$

Instead, simplify the denominator first:

$$\frac{5}{15+10} = \frac{5}{25} = \frac{1}{5}$$

The terms in example (c) may not be split either:

$$\frac{15+10}{5+2} \neq \frac{15}{5} + \frac{10}{2} \quad \textbf{NO!}$$

Instead, simplify both parts of the fraction:

$$\frac{15+10}{5+2} = \frac{25}{7} = 3\frac{4}{7}$$

Often, GMAT problems will involve complex fractions with variables. On these problems, it is tempting to split the denominator. Do not fall for it!

$$\frac{5x-2y}{x-y} \neq \frac{5x}{x} - \frac{2y}{y}$$

The reality is that $\frac{5x-2y}{x-y}$ cannot be simplified further, because neither of the terms in the numerator shares a factor with the entire denominator.

On the other hand, the expression $\frac{6x-15y}{10}$ can be simplified by splitting the numerator. Both terms in the numerator share a factor with the denominator, and by splitting into two fractions, you can write each part in simplified form:

$$\frac{6x-15y}{10} = \frac{6x}{10} - \frac{15y}{10} = \frac{3x}{5} - \frac{3y}{2}$$

Problem Set

For problems #1–5, decide whether the given operation will cause the original value to **increase**, **decrease**, or **stay the same**.

1. Multiply the numerator of a positive, proper fraction by $\dfrac{3}{2}$.

2. Add 1 to the numerator of a positive, proper fraction and subtract 1 from its denominator.

3. Multiply both the numerator and denominator of a positive, proper fraction by $3\dfrac{1}{2}$.

4. Multiply a positive, proper fraction by $\dfrac{3}{8}$.

5. Divide a positive, proper fraction by $\dfrac{3}{13}$.

Solve problems 6–10.

6. Simplify: $\dfrac{10x}{5+x}$

7. Simplify: $\dfrac{8(3)(x)^2(3)}{6x}$

8. Simplify: $\dfrac{\dfrac{3}{5}+\dfrac{1}{3}}{\dfrac{2}{3}+\dfrac{2}{5}}$

9. Simplify: $\dfrac{12ab^3-6a^2b}{3ab}$ (given that $ab \neq 0$)

10. Are $\dfrac{\sqrt{3}}{2}$ and $\dfrac{2\sqrt{3}}{3}$ reciprocals?

Solutions

1. **Increase:** Multiplying the numerator of a positive fraction by a number greater than 1 increases the numerator. As the numerator of a positive, proper fraction increases, its value increases.

2. **Increase:** As the numerator of a positive, proper fraction increases, the value of the fraction increases. As the denominator of a positive, proper fraction decreases, the value of the fraction also increases. Both actions will work to increase the value of the fraction.

3. **Stay the same:** Multiplying or dividing the numerator and denominator of a fraction by the same number will not change the value of the fraction.

4. **Decrease:** Multiplying a positive number by a proper fraction decreases the number.

5. **Increase:** Dividing a positive number by a positive, proper fraction increases the number.

6. **Cannot simplify:** There is no way to simplify this fraction; it is already in simplest form. Remember, you cannot split the denominator!

7. **12x:** First, cancel terms in both the numerator and the denominator. Then combine terms:

$$\frac{8(3)(x)^2(3)}{6x} = \frac{8(3)(x)^2(3)}{6\,2x} = \frac{8\,4(x)^2(3)}{2x} = \frac{4(x)^2(3)}{x} = 4(x)(3) = 12x$$

8. $\dfrac{7}{8}$ **:** First, add the fractions in the numerator and denominator:

$$\frac{\dfrac{14}{15}}{\dfrac{16}{15}} = \frac{\overset{7}{14}}{15} \times \frac{\overset{1}{15}}{16_8} = \frac{7}{8}$$

Alternatively, to save time, multiply each of the small fractions by 15, which is the common denominator of all the fractions in the problem. Because you are multiplying the numerator *and* the denominator of the whole complex fraction by 15, you are not changing its value:

$$\frac{9+5}{10+6} = \frac{14}{16} = \frac{7}{8}$$

9. **2($2b^2 - a$) or $4b^2 - 2a$:** First, factor out common terms in the numerator. Then, cancel terms in both the numerator and denominator:

$$\frac{6ab(2b^2 - a)}{3ab} = 2(2b^2 - a) \text{ or } 4b^2 - 2a$$

10. **Yes:** The product of a number and its reciprocal must equal 1. To test whether or not two numbers are reciprocals, multiply them. If the product is 1, they are reciprocals; if it is not, they are not:

$$\frac{\sqrt{3}}{2} \times \frac{2\sqrt{3}}{3} = \frac{2\left(\sqrt{3}\right)^2}{2(3)} = \frac{6}{6} = 1$$

Thus, the numbers are indeed reciprocals.

4

MANHATTAN
PREP

Chapter 5

of

Fractions, Decimals, & Percents

Percents

In This Chapter...

Chapter 5

Percents

The third component of the FDP trifecta is percents. Percent literally means "per one hundred." You can think of a percent as simply a special type of fraction or decimal that involves the number 100:

> 75% of the students like chocolate ice cream.

This means that, out of every 100 students, 75 like chocolate ice cream.

In fraction form, you write this as 75/100, which simplifies to 3/4.

In decimal form, you write this as 0.75.

One common mistake is the belief that 100% equals 100. This is not correct. In fact, 100% means 100/100. Therefore, 100% = 1.

Percents as Decimals: Multiplication Shortcut

You can convert percents into decimals by moving the decimal point two spaces to the left:

$$525\% = 5.25 \qquad 52.5\% = 0.525 \qquad 5.25\% = 0.0525 \qquad 0.525\% = 0.00525$$

A decimal can be converted into a percent by moving the decimal point two spaces to the right:

$$0.6 = 60\% \qquad 0.28 = 28\% \qquad 0.459 = 45.9\% \qquad 1.3 = 130\%$$

Strategy Tip: Remember, the percent is always "bigger" than the decimal!

Percent, Of, Is, What

These four words are by far the most important when translating percent questions. In fact, many percent word problems can be rephrased in terms of these four words:

Percent	=	divide by 100	(/100)
Of	=	multiply	(×)
Is	=	equals	(=)
What	=	unknown value	(x, y, or any variable)

What is 70 percent of 120?

As you read left to right, translate the question into an equation:

x	=	70	/100	×	120
What	is	70	percent	of	120?

Now solve the equation:

$$x = \frac{70}{100} \times 120$$
$$x = \frac{7}{10} \times 120$$
$$x = 7 \times 12$$
$$x = 84$$

This translation works no matter what order the words appear in.

30 is what percent of 50?

This statement can be translated directly into an equation:

30	=	x	/100	×	50
30	is	what	percent	of	50?

Every time you create one of these equations, your goal is the same: Solve for the unknown.

In the above examples, x represents the unknown value that you have been asked to find. By isolating x, you will answer the question:

$$30 = \frac{x}{100} \times 50$$
$$30 = \frac{x}{2}$$
$$60 = x$$

Look for Percent, Of, Is, and What as you translate percent problems into equations; those four words should provide the necessary structure for each equation. As you get better with translation, you may feel comfortable using a shortcut when the problem asks *30 is what percent of 50*? You can always translate this form as:

$$\frac{30}{50} = x\%$$

Quick Calculations: Building Percents

You can calculate most percentages quickly using a combination of 50%, 10%, 5%, and 1% of the original number.

For example, the previous section asked you to find 70% of 120. Note that 70% is the equivalent of 50% + 10% + 10%. It is much easier to calculate 50% and 10% of a number:

100% (original number)	50%	10%	50% + 10% + 10% = 70%
120	60	12	60 + 12 + 12 = 84

Likewise, to calculate 15% of a number, add 10% and 5%:

What is 15% of 90?

100% = 90
10% = 9
 5% = 4.5
15% = 9 + 4.5 = 13.5

Test your skills on these drills:

1. What is 7% of 50?
2. What is 40% of 30?
3. What is 75% of 20?

Here are the answers:

1. 100% = 50
   5% = 2.5 (10% = 5, so 5% = half of that)
   1% = 0.5
   7% = 5% + 1% + 1% = 2.5 + 0.5 + 0.5 = 3.5

2. 100% = 30
   10% = 3
   40% = (4)(10%) = (4)(3) = 12

3. Don't forget about your fraction-conversion skills! Sometimes, it's easier to convert to fractions and cancel: $75\% = \dfrac{3}{4}$.

$$\frac{3}{\cancel{4}_1}(\cancel{20}^5) = (3)(5) = 15$$

Why is it (arguably) easier to use the **building percents** method on the first two problems, but easier to use fractions on the third problem?

Most people don't memorize the fraction conversion for 7%, so the first problem is definitely easier to build via percents.

The second problem could go either way, but because 40% is a multiple of 10%, and 10% is very easy to find, building the answer is quick.

In the third problem, 75% would take multiple steps to build via the percent method. It turns out that 75% also converts to a very nice fraction: $\dfrac{3}{4}$. In this case, it will probably be easier to use the fraction here (especially because the starting number, 20, is a multiple of 4, so the denominator will cancel entirely!).

Percent Increase and Decrease

Consider this example:

> The price of a cup of coffee increased from 80 cents to 84 cents. By what percent did the price change?

If you want to find a change, whether in terms of percent or of actual value, use the following equation:

$$\textbf{Percent Change} = \frac{\textbf{Change in Value}}{\textbf{Original Value}}$$

In the coffee example, you want to find the *change* in terms of percent. Write $\dfrac{x}{100}$ to represent an unknown percent:

$$\% \text{ Change} = \frac{\text{Change}}{\text{Original}}$$

$$\frac{x}{100} = \frac{4}{80} = \frac{1}{20}$$

$$20x = 100$$

$$x = 5$$

Therefore, the price has been increased 5%.

Alternatively, a question might ask:

If the price of a $30 shirt is decreased by 20%, what is the final price of the shirt?

In this case, the question didn't tell you the new percent; rather, it gave the percent decrease. If the price decreases by 20%, then the new price is 100% − 20% = 80% of the original. Use the new percent, not the decrease in percent, to solve for the new price directly. You can use this equation:

$$\text{New Percent} = \frac{\text{New Value}}{\text{Original Value}}$$

Once again, use *x* to represent the value you want, the new price:

$$\frac{80}{100} = \frac{x}{30}$$

$$\frac{4}{5} = \frac{x}{30}$$

$$\frac{4}{1} = \frac{x}{6}$$

$$24 = x$$

The new price of the shirt is $24.

Alternatively, you can solve directly without setting up a proportion. The starting price is $30 and this price is decreased by 20%. Find 20% of $30 and subtract:

$30 − (20\%)($30)   20% of 30 is 6
$30 − $6 = $24

Increasing or Decreasing from the Original

The language on the GMAT can sometimes be confusing. The original number is the starting point for a comparison. For example, if a problem asks how much smaller the population was in 1980 than in

1990, then the 1990 population is the starting point, or original number. When talking about a percent change made to a number, always think of the original number as 100%.

For example, if you increase a number by 10%, then the new number will be 110% of the original number. Here are some common language cues for this concept:

> 10% increase = 110% of the original
> 10% greater than = 110% of the original

If you decrease a number, then you subtract from 100%:

> 45% decrease = 55% of the original
> 45% less than = 55% of the original

Use this conversion to save steps on percent problems. For example:

> **What number is 50% greater than 60?**

50% greater than is the same as *150% of.* Rewrite the question:

> **What number is 150% of 60?**

Translate into an equation, using 1.5 to represent 150%:

> $x = 1.5 \times 60$
> $x = 90$

Successive Percent Change

Some problems will ask you to calculate successive percents. For example:

> **If a ticket increased in price by 20%, and then increased again by 5%, by what percent did the ticket price increase in total?**

Although it may seem counterintuitive, the answer is *not 25%*.

Walk through this with real numbers. If the ticket originally cost $100, then the first increase would bring the ticket price up to 100 plus 20% of 100 (or $20) for a total of $120.

The second increase of 5% is now based on this *new* ticket price, $120:

> $120 + (0.05)(120) = \$126$

The price increased from $100 to $126, so the percent increase is the change divided by the original, or $\dfrac{26}{100} = 26\%$.

Successive percents *cannot* simply be added together; instead, you have to calculate each piece separately. This holds for successive increases, successive decreases, and for combinations of increases and decreases.

Try this problem:

> The cost of a plane ticket is increased by 25%. Later, the ticket goes on sale and the price is reduced 20%. What is the overall percent change in the price of the ticket?

You can *multiply* these changes together; you can't just add or subtract them. A 25% increase followed by a 20% decrease is the same as 125% of 80% of the original number:

$$\left(\frac{125}{100}\right)\left(\frac{80}{100}\right)x =$$

$$\left(\frac{5}{4}\right)\left(\frac{4}{5}\right)x = x$$

The 20% decrease entirely offsets the 25% increase. The new price is exactly the same as the original price. You can also work through the math using a real number, as shown in the previous problem:

$100 + (25\% \text{ of } \$100) = \$125$

$125 - (20\% \text{ of } \$125) = \$100$

Interest Formulas

Certain GMAT problems require a working knowledge of compound interest. If you struggle to memorize formulas and are not looking for an 85th percentile or higher Quant score, you may be able to skip memorizing the formula. Instead, learn how to do some of the easier problems and guess if you hit a harder one.

$$\textbf{Total Amount} = P\left(1+\frac{r}{n}\right)^{nt}$$

In this equation, P = principal, r = rate (in decimal form), n = number of times per year, and t = number of years.

Some of these can be solved as successive percents problems:

> A bank account with $200 earns 5% annual interest, compounded annually. If there are no deposits or withdrawals, how much money will the account have after 2 years?

First, calculate how many times the interest will compound. It compounds once a year for 2 years, so it will compound twice.

If the account earns 5% interest, that is an increase of 5% each year. In other words, the new value of the account is 105% of 105% of $200.

At the end of the first year, the account will have $200 + 5% of $200. Calculate 5% by taking 10% of $200 and then dividing by 2 to get $10:

200	20	10
starting number	10% of starting number	5% of starting number

At the end of the first, year, then, the account will have $210.

For the second year, your starting point is $210. At the end of the second year, the account will have: $210 + (0.05)(210) = 210 + 10.5 = 220.50. (You can use the same procedure to find 5% here. Also, notice that the total increase is just a little bit more than it would have been without compounding. It would take a lot of compounding periods to make a big difference. This can be important if you're trying to narrow down the answer choices.)

If the interest compounds quarterly, the process is the same, although there is one extra step. For example:

> A bank account with $100 earns 8% annual interest, compounded quarterly. If there are no deposits or withdrawals. how much money will be in the account after 6 months?

First, figure out how many times the interest compounds. If the interest compounds quarterly, it compounds every 3 months. In 6 months, the interest will compound twice.

Next, the 8% interest is spread evenly throughout the year. The interest compounds 4 times each year, so each time it compounds at one-fourth of the total interest.

In other words, each time it compounds, there is a 2% increase. After 6 months, the new value of the account will be 102% of 102% of $100:

At the end of the first quarter, the account will have $100 plus 2% of $100. Calculate 2% by finding 1% and multiplying by 2:

100	1	2
starting number	1% of starting number	2% of starting number

At the end of the first quarter, the account will have $102.

At the end of the second quarter, the account will have: $102 + (0.02)(102) = 102 + 2.04 = 104.04. (You can use the same procedure to find 2% here.)

For shorter calculations, you can avoid the compound interest formula by treating the problem as a successive percent change problem.

Problem Set

1. A stereo was marked down by 30% and sold for $84. What was the presale price of the stereo?

2. A car loan is offered at 8% annual interest, compounded annually. After the first year, the interest due is $240. What is the principal on the loan?

3. *x* is 40% of *y*. 50% of *y* is 40. 16 is what percent of *x*?

4. A bowl is half full of water. Four cups of water are then added to the bowl, filling the bowl to 70% of its capacity. How many cups of water are now in the bowl?

5. Company X has exactly two product lines and no other sources of revenue. If the consumer product line experiences a *k*% increase in revenue (where *k* is a positive integer) in 2015 from 2014 levels and the machine parts line experiences a *k*% decrease in revenue in 2015 from 2014 levels, did Company X's overall revenue increase or decrease in 2015?

    (1) In 2014, the consumer products line generated more revenue than the machine parts line.
    (2) *k* = 8

Save the below problem set for review, either after you finish this book or after you finish all of the Quant books that you plan to study.

6. 800, increased by 50% and then decreased by 30%, yields what number?

7. If 1,500 is increased by 20% and then reduced by *y*%, yielding 1,080, what is *y*?

8. A bottle is 80% full. The liquid in the bottle consists of 60% guava juice and 40% pineapple juice. The remainder of the bottle is then filled with 200 mL of rum. How much guava juice is in the bottle?

9. Company Z only sells chairs and tables. What percent of its revenue in 2008 did Company Z derive from its sales of chairs?

    (1) In 2008, the price of tables sold by Company Z was 10% higher than the price of chairs sold by Company Z.
    (2) In 2008, Company Z sold 20% fewer tables than chairs.

Solutions

1. **$120:** You know the new price of the stereo, so you can use the following formula:

$$\text{New Percent} = \frac{\text{New Value}}{\text{Original Value}}$$

The new value of the stereo is $84. If the price of the stereo was marked down 30%, then the new percent is $100 - 30 = 70\%$. Finally, the original value is the value you're asked for, so you can replace it with x:

$$\frac{70}{100} = \frac{84}{x}$$
$$\frac{7}{10} = \frac{84}{x}$$
$$7x = 840$$
$$x = 120$$

Alternatively, you could rephrase the given information to say the following:

$84 is 70% of the original price of the stereo.

You could then translate this statement into an equation and solve:

$$84 = \left(\frac{70}{100}\right)x$$
$$84 = \left(\frac{7}{10}\right)x$$
$$840 = 7x$$
$$120 = x$$

2. **$3,000:** Although this looks like an interest problem, you can think of it as a percent change problem. The percent change is 8%, and the change in value is $240:

$$\text{Percent Change} = \frac{\text{Change in Value}}{\text{Original Value}}$$
$$\frac{8}{100} = \frac{240}{x}$$
$$8x = 24,000$$
$$x = 3,000$$

The principal amount of the loan is $3,000.

Alternatively, you could rephrase the given information to say the following:

$240 is 8% of the total loan.

You could then translate this statement into an equation and solve:

$$240 = \left(\frac{8}{100}\right)x$$
$$24{,}000 = 8x$$
$$3{,}000 = x$$

3. **50%:** You can translate the first two sentences directly into equations:

x is 40% of y → $x = \left(\dfrac{40}{100}\right)y$

50% of y is 40   → $\left(\dfrac{50}{100}\right)y = 40$

You can solve the second equation for y:

$$\left(\frac{50}{100}\right)y = 40$$
$$\left(\frac{1}{2}\right)y = 40$$
$$y = 80$$

Now you can replace y with 80 in the first equation to solve for x:

$$x = \left(\frac{40}{100}\right)(80)$$
$$x = \frac{4}{10} \times 80$$
$$x = 4 \times 8 = 32$$

Be careful now. The question asks, "16 is what percent of x?"

You know that $x = 32$, so this question is really asking, "16 is what percent of 32?"

Create a new variable (z) to represent the unknown value in the question and solve:

$$16 = \frac{z}{100} \times 32$$
$$16 \times \frac{100}{32} = z$$
$$1 \times \frac{100}{2} = z$$
$$50 = z$$

Thus, 16 is 50% of x.

MANHATTAN
PREP

4. **14 cups of water:** If the bowl was already half full of water, then it was originally 50% full. Adding 4 cups of water increased the percentage by 20% of the total capacity of the bowl.

You can use the percent change formula to solve for the total capacity of the bowl:

$$\text{Percent Change} = \frac{\text{Change in Value}}{\text{Original Value}}$$

$$\frac{20}{100} = \frac{4}{x}$$

$$\frac{1}{5} = \frac{4}{x}$$

$$x = 20$$

The total capacity of the bowl is 20 cups, but the question asks for the total number of cups currently in the bowl. You know the bowl is 70% full. You can ask the question, "What is 70% of 20?" and solve:

$$x = \frac{70}{100} \times 20$$

$$x = \frac{7}{10} \times 20$$

$$10x = 140$$

$$x = 14$$

There are 14 cups of water in the bowl.

Alternatively, you can save time by solving directly for 70% rather than by first solving for the full capacity. You know 4 represents 20% of the capacity. Let x represent 70% of the capacity. Set up a proportion and solve for x:

$$\frac{4}{x} = \frac{20}{70}$$

$$\frac{4}{x} = \frac{2}{7}$$

$$28 = 2x$$

$$14 = x$$

5. **(A):** This question requires you to employ logic about percents. No calculation is required, or even possible.

Here's what you know so far (use new variables c and m to keep track of your information):

2014:

        consumer products makes c dollars
        machine parts makes m dollars
        total revenue $= c + m$

2015:

> consumer products makes "c dollars increased by $k\%$"
>
> machine parts makes "m dollars decreased by $k\%$"
>
> total revenue = ?

What would you need to answer the question, "Did Company X's overall revenue increase or decrease in 2015?" Certainly, if you knew the values of c, m, and k, you could achieve sufficiency, but the GMAT would never write such an easy problem. What is the *minimum* you would need to know to answer definitively?

Since both changes involve the same percent (k), you know that c increases *by the same percent* by which m decreases. So, you don't actually need to know k. You already know that k percent of whichever number is greater (c or m) will constitute a bigger change to the overall revenue.

All this question is asking is whether the overall revenue went up or down. If c started off greater, then a $k\%$ increase in c means more new dollars coming in than you would lose due to a $k\%$ decrease in the smaller number, m. If c is smaller, then the $k\%$ increase would be smaller than what you would lose due to a $k\%$ decrease in the larger number, m.

The question can be rephrased, "Which is greater, c or m?"

(1) SUFFICIENT: This statement tells you that c is greater than m. Thus, a $k\%$ increase in c is greater than a $k\%$ decrease in m, and the overall revenue went up.

(2) INSUFFICIENT: Knowing the percent change doesn't help, since you don't know whether c or m is bigger.

Note that you could plug in real numbers if you wanted to, although the problem is faster with logic. Using statement (1) only:

2014:

> consumer products makes $200
>
> machine parts makes $100
>
> total revenue = $300

2015: *if k = 50*

> consumer products makes $300
>
> machine parts makes $50
>
> total revenue = $350

This yields an answer of yes—the overall revenue did increase. However, you might have to test several sets of numbers to establish that this will always be true. (That's the main reason that logic is faster here!) You can experiment with different values for c and m, and you can change k to any positive

5

integer (you don't need to know what k is). As long as c is greater than m, you will get the same result. The increase to the larger c will be greater than the decrease to the smaller m.

The correct answer is **(A)**.

6. **840:** This is a successive percent question. 800 increased by 50% and decreased by 30% is the same as 150% of 70% of 800:

$$\frac{150}{100} \times \frac{70}{100} \times 800 =$$
$$\frac{3}{2} \times \frac{7}{10} \times 800 =$$
$$\frac{21}{20} \times 800 =$$
$$21 \times 40 = 840$$

7. **40:** Break the question into two parts.

First, 1,500 is increased by 20%. Thus, 120% percent of 1,500 is:

$$\left(\frac{120}{100}\right)1,500 =$$
$$\left(\frac{6}{5}\right)1,500 =$$
$$(6)300 = 1,800$$

You are solving for y, which represents the percent change of 1,800:

$$\text{Percent Change} = \frac{\text{Change in Value}}{\text{Original Value}}$$

The change in value from 1,800 to 1,080 is $1,800 - 1,080 = 720$:

$$\frac{y}{100} = \frac{720}{1,800}$$

You can save time by noticing that 720 and 1,800 are both divisible by 360:

$$\frac{y}{100} = \frac{2}{5}$$
$$y = \frac{200}{5} = 40$$

8. **480 mL**: You can begin by figuring out what the total amount of liquid is.

If the bottle was 80% full, and adding 200 mL of rum made the bottle full, then 200 mL is equal to 20% of the total capacity of the bottle. Let b be the total capacity of the bottle:

$$200 = \frac{20}{100}b$$
$$200 = \frac{1}{5}b$$
$$1{,}000 = b$$

The bottle has a total capacity of 1,000 mL.

Now you can use a successive percent to figure out the total amount of guava juice. You know 80% of the bottle is filled with juice, and 60% of the juice is guava juice. In other words, guava juice is 60% of 80% of 1,000 mL:

$$g = \left(\frac{60}{100}\right)\left(\frac{80}{100}\right)1{,}000$$
$$g = \left(\frac{3}{5}\right)\left(\frac{4}{5}\right)1{,}000$$
$$g = \left(\frac{3}{1}\right)\left(\frac{4}{1}\right)40$$
$$g = 3 \times 160$$
$$g = 480$$

There is 480 mL of guava juice.

Note that the last calculation, $3 \times 4 \times 40$, can be done in any order that is easiest for you. Most of the time, multiplying the largest numbers together first is easier in the long run

9. **(C):** First of all, notice that the question is only asking for the *percent* of its revenue the company derived from chairs. The question is asking for a relative value.

The revenue for the company can be expressed by the following equation:

$$\text{Revenue}_{\text{Company Z}} = R_T + R_C$$

If you can find the relative value of *any* two of these revenues, you will have enough information to answer the question.

Also, note that the GMAT will expect you to know that Revenue = Price × Quantity Sold. This relationship is discussed in more detail in Chapter 1 of the *Word Problems GMAT Strategy Guide*.

The revenue derived from tables is the price per table multiplied by the number of tables sold. The revenue derived from chairs is the price per chair multiplied by the number of chairs sold. You can create some variables to represent these unknown values:

$$R_T = P_T \times Q_T$$
$$R_C = P_C \times Q_C$$

(1) INSUFFICIENT: This statement gives you the relative value of the price of tables to the price of chairs. If the price of tables was 10% higher than the price of chairs, then the price of tables was 110% of the price of chairs:

$$P_T = 1.1P_C$$

However, without any information on quantity, this information by itself does not give you the relative value of their revenues.

(2) INSUFFICIENT: If the company sold 20% fewer tables than chairs, then the number of tables sold is 80% of the number of chairs sold:

$$Q_T = 0.8Q_C$$

This information by itself, without any information about price, does not give you the relative value of their revenues.

(1) AND (2) SUFFICIENT: Look again at the equation for revenue derived from the sale of tables:

$$R_T = P_T \times Q_T$$

Replace P_T with $1.1P_C$ and replace Q_T with $0.8Q_C$:

$$P_T \times Q_T = (1.1P_C) \times (0.8Q_C)$$
$$P_T \times Q_T = (0.88)(P_C \times Q_C)$$
$$R_T = (0.88)R_C$$

Taken together, the two statements provide the relative value of the revenues. No further calculation is required to know that you *can* find the percent of revenue generated from the sale of chairs. In fact, if you know that you can relate tables to chairs in terms of both quantity and price, it isn't even necessary to calculate revenue at all. The statements together are sufficient.

If you do want to perform the calculation, it would look something like this:

$$\frac{R_C}{\text{Total Revenue}} = \frac{R_C}{R_T + R_C} = \frac{R_C}{(0.88)R_C + R_C} = \frac{\cancel{R_C}}{(1.88)\cancel{R_C}} = \frac{1}{1.88} \approx 53\%$$

Save time on Data Sufficiency questions by avoiding unnecessary computation. Once you know you can find the percent, stop and move on to the next problem.

The correct answer is **(C)**.

Chapter 6
of
Fractions, Decimals, & Percents

Strategy: Choose Smart Numbers

In This Chapter...

Chapter 6

Strategy: Choose Smart Numbers

Some algebra problems—problems that involve unknowns, or variables—can be turned into arithmetic problems instead. Such problems are commonly tested with fractions, percents, and even ratios. You're better at arithmetic than algebra (everybody is!), so turning an annoying variable-based problem into one that uses real numbers can save time and aggravation on the GMAT.

Which of the below two problems is easier for you to solve?

50% of 10% of a number is what percent of that number?

50% of 10% of 100 is what percent of 100?

(A) 1%   (B) 5%   (C) 10%

(A) 1%   (B) 5%   (C) 10%

In the first problem, you would assign a variable to the unknown *number* mentioned, and then you would use algebra to solve. You may think that this version is not particularly difficult, but no matter how easy you think it is, it's still easier to work with real numbers.

The set-up of the two problems is identical—and this feature is at the heart of how you can turn algebra into arithmetic.

How Do Smart Numbers Work?

Here's how to solve the algebra version of the above problem using smart numbers:

Step 1: *Choose smart numbers* to replace the unknowns.

How do you know you can choose a random number in the first place? The problem talks about a number but never supplies a real value for that number anywhere in the problem or in the answers. If you were to do this problem algebraically, you would have to assign a variable.

Instead, choose a real number. In general, 100 is a great number to choose on percent problems.

Step 2: Solve the problem using your chosen smart numbers.

Wherever the problem talks about the *number*, assume it now says 100:

50% of 10% of 100 is what percent of 100?

Do the math! 50% of 100 is 50; 10% of 50 is 5. Therefore, the question is asking: 5 is what percent of 100?

Now you can see the beauty of starting with 100 on a percent problem: $\dfrac{5}{100} = 5\%$. You don't actually have to convert to a percent in the end!

Step 3: Find a match in the answers.

The correct answer is **(B)**.

FDP smart numbers problems can appear with percents, fractions, or ratios in the answers, in which case you'll use the three-step process shown above. Problems can also appear with variables in the answers, in which that third step (find a match) will take a little more work. You'll try one of these later in this chapter.

Smart Numbers with Percents

It's crucial to know when you're allowed to use this technique. It's also crucial to know how *you* are going to decide whether to use textbook math or to choose smart numbers; you will typically have time to try just one of the two techniques during your 2 minutes on the problem.

The *choose smart numbers* technique can be used any time a problem contains only *unspecified* values. The easiest example of such a problem is one that contains variables, percents, fractions, or ratios throughout. It does not provide real numbers for those variables, even in the answer choices. Whenever a problem has this characteristic, you can choose your own smart numbers to turn the problem into arithmetic.

There is some cost to doing so: it can take extra time compared to the "pure" textbook solution. As a result, the technique is most useful when the problem is a hard one for you. If you find the abstract math involved to be very easy, then you may not want to take the time to transform the problem into arithmetic. As the math gets more complicated, however, the arithmetic form becomes comparatively easier and faster to use. For instance, in the initial example, maybe you quickly saw that 50% of 10% is equal to 5%, and you didn't see the need for smart numbers. Don't let this put you off of using the strategy when the going gets tough. Test-takers at every level are likely to encounter at least a few problems that are much easier to solve with real numbers than with unknowns.

MANHATTAN
PREP

Try this problem using smart numbers:

> The price of a certain computer is increased by 10%, and then the new price is increased by an additional 5%. The new price is what percent of the original price?
>
> (A) 120%
> (B) 115.5%
> (C) 115%
> (D) 112.5%
> (E) 110%

First, how do you know that you can choose smart numbers on this problem? The problem talks about the price of a computer but never mentions a real number for that price anywhere along the way.

Step 1: Choose smart numbers.

This percent problem doesn't already use 100, so choose 100 for the starting price of the computer.

Step 2: Solve.

First, the computer's price is increased by 10%, so the new price is: $100 + $10 = $110. Next, the *new* price is increased by a further 5%, so the price becomes: $110 + (0.05)($110) = $110 + $5.50 = $115.50.

The new price is $115.50 and the original price is $100, so $\dfrac{115.50}{100}$ equals 115.5%. In other words, you can ignore the denominator; your final number already represents the desired percent.

Step 3: Find a match.

(A) 120%
(B) 115.5% → match
(C) 115%
(D) 112.5%
(E) 110%

The correct answer is **(B)**. Notice that the answer is just slightly larger than you'd get if you simply increased the price by 15%.

Let's say that you weren't able to choose $100 for some reason. Instead, you chose an initial price of $20. How would the problem work? Try it out before continuing to read.

If the initial price is $20, then the first increase of 10% would bring the price to: $20 + $2 = $22. The next increase of 5% would bring the price to: $22 + (0.05)($22) = $22 + $1.1 = $23.10.

Tip: to calculate 5% quickly, first find 10% of the desired number, then halve the number.

For example, to find 5% of 22, first find 10%: 2.2. Then halve that number: $\dfrac{2.2}{2} = 1.1$.

Now what? $23.10 isn't in the answers. Remember that you didn't start with 100! The new price as a percent of the original is $\dfrac{23.10}{20}$. How do you turn that into a percent?

First, remember that percent means "per 100." Manipulate the fraction until you get 100 on the bottom.

$$\frac{23.10}{20} \times \frac{5}{5} = \frac{115.5}{100}$$

The answer is 115.5%.

That last calculation is annoying—you don't want to do it unless you have to. Therefore, if you *can* pick 100 on a percent problem, do so.

Smart Numbers with Fractions

Try this problem:

Two libraries are planning to combine a portion of their collections in one new space.

$\dfrac{1}{3}$ of the books from Library A will be housed in the new space, along with $\dfrac{1}{4}$ of the books from Library B. If there are twice as many books in Library B as in Library A, what proportion of the books in the new space will have come from Library A?

(A) $\dfrac{1}{3}$

(B) $\dfrac{2}{5}$

(C) $\dfrac{1}{2}$

(D) $\dfrac{3}{5}$

(E) $\dfrac{7}{12}$

Step 1: Choose smart numbers.

When working with fraction problems, choose a common denominator of the fractions given in the problem. In this case, the problem contains the fractions $\dfrac{1}{3}$ and $\dfrac{1}{4}$, so use the common denominator of 12.

Note two things. First, technically, any multiple of 12 will work nicely, but keep things simple: use the smallest common denominator possible.

MANHATTAN
PREP

Second, what should you call 12? All of the books from Library A? Or from Library B? The number of books that will be moved from Library A to the new space? Or from Library B to the new space?

Assign the value 12 to the total for the smaller library—in this case, Library A—because the other library has twice as many books. That is, Library B's capacity, 24, is a multiple of Library A's capacity; Library B's capacity is also a multiple of the denominators 3 and 4.

Step 2: Solve.

If Library A has 12 books total, then Library B must have 24 books total.

$\dfrac{1}{3}$ of Library A's books, or $(12)\left(\dfrac{1}{3}\right) = 4$, will move to the new space.

$\dfrac{1}{4}$ of Library B's books, or $(24)\left(\dfrac{1}{4}\right) = 6$, will move to the new space.

The new space will therefore contain 10 books total. Because 4 out of 10 of those books came from Library A, 40%, or $\dfrac{2}{5}$ of the books in the new space will have come from Library A.

Step 3: Find a match.

The correct answer is **(B)**.

Bonus Exercise: Take a look at the wrong answers. Can you figure out how someone would have gotten to any of them?

Answer (A), $\dfrac{1}{3}$, is the original figure given for the portion of Library A's books moved to the new space. This represents the moved books as a proportion of the original library's capacity, not the new space's capacity.

Answer (D), $\dfrac{3}{5}$, represents the proportion of Library B's books in the new space. If you calculated this answer, then you solved for the wrong thing.

Answer (E), $\dfrac{7}{12}$, represents the sum of $\dfrac{1}{3}$ and $\dfrac{1}{4}$. You can't just add up the two starting fractions, however, because the two libraries have a different number of books to start.

Smart Numbers with Variables in the Answers

This same strategy works when there are variables, rather than percents or fractions, in the answers. However, you'll have to add one more piece to the third step.

Try this problem:

> The Crandall's hot tub has a capacity of x liters and is half full. Their swimming pool, which has a capacity of y liters, is filled to four-fifths of its capacity. If enough water is drained from the swimming pool to fill the hot tub to capacity, the pool is now how many liters short of full capacity, in terms of x and y?
>
> (A) $0.8y - 0.5x$
> (B) $0.8y + 0.5x$
> (C) $0.2y + 0.5x$
> (D) $0.3(y - x)$
> (E) $0.3(y + x)$

Step 1: Choose smart numbers.

The problem keeps talking about the capacity of the hot tub and pool but never offers a real number for either. Instead, it introduces the variables x and y, which also appear in the answers. You can use smart numbers on this problem.

The two variables are not connected (that is, once you pick one, the other one is not automatically determined), so you'll have to pick two numbers. Pick something divisible by 2 for x and divisible by 5 for y:

$$x = 4 \text{ and } y = 20$$

Step 2: Solve.

The hot tub, with a capacity of 4, is half full, so there are 2 liters of water in the hot tub. The pool, with a capacity of 20, is four-fifths full, so there are 16 liters in the pool.

The hot tub needs another 2 liters to be full, so the pool will have to lose 2 liters; the pool is now down to 14 liters. Since its total capacity is 20, the pool is 6 liters short of capacity.

Step 3: Find a match.

When the answers contain variables, you have to add an intermediate step: plug your starting values, $x = 4$ and $y = 20$, into the answers to find the match:

(A) $0.8y - 0.5x = (0.8)(20) - (0.5)(4) = 16 - 2 = 14$

(B) $0.8y + 0.5x = (0.8)(20) + (0.5)(4) =$ too big, since (A) was too big

(C) $0.2y + 0.5x = (0.2)(20) + (0.5)(4) = 4 + 2 = 6$ Match!

(D) $0.3(y - x) = 0.3(20 - 4) = 0.3(16) =$ not an integer

(E) $0.3(y + x) = 0.3(20+4) = 0.3(24) =$ not an integer

The correct answer is (**C**).

Note that some of the work shown above seems to be incomplete; that is, each answer was not calculated fully. Your goal is to find a match; in this case, you want to find the answer that matches 6. You do not actually need to figure out the value of each answer. As soon as you can tell that the value will *not* be 6, stop and cross off that answer.

When the answers contain variables, there is one potential problem to watch for when you choose smart numbers. In certain circumstances, the number(s) you choose will work for more than one answer choice. In that case, you can guess and move on, but it's generally not too hard to adjust by changing one of your numbers and seeing which answer choice still works.

If you follow the guidelines for choosing numbers, you will greatly reduce the chances that your smart number(s) will work for more than one answer:

- Do not pick 0 or 1.
- Do not pick numbers that appear elsewhere in the problem.
- If you have to choose multiple numbers, choose different numbers, ideally with different properties (e.g., odd and even). The above case used even numbers for both due to the fractions mentioned in the problem, but note that the numbers chosen were fairly far apart.

To summarize the choose smart numbers strategy:

Step 0: Recognize that you can choose smart numbers.

The problem talks about some values but doesn't provide real numbers for those values. Rather, it uses variables or only refers to fractions or percents. The answer choices consist of variable expressions, fractions, or percents.

Step 1: Choose smart numbers.

Follow all constraints given in the problem. If the problem says that x is odd, pick an odd number for x. If the problem says that $x + y = z$, then note that once you pick for x and y, you have to calculate z. Don't pick your own random number for z! Pay attention to the following:

- If you have to pick for more than one variable, pick different numbers for each one. If possible, pick numbers with different characteristics (e.g., one even and one odd).

- Follow any constraints given in the problem. You may be restricted to positive numbers or to integers, for example, depending upon the way the problem is worded.

- Avoid choosing 0, 1, or numbers that already appear in the problem.

- Choose numbers that work easily in the problem. Typically, 100 is often the best number to use for percent problems. On fraction problems, try the common denominator of any fractions that appear in the problem.

Step 2: Solve the problem using your chosen smart numbers.

Wherever the problem used to have variables or unknowns, read the problem as though it now contains the real numbers that you've chosen. Solve the problem arithmetically and find your target answer.

Step 3: Find a match in the answers.

1. Pick the matching fraction or percent in the answers, or

2. plug your smart numbers into the variables in the answer choices and look for the choice that matches your target. If, at any point, you can tell that a particular answer will *not* match your target, stop calculating that answer. Cross it off and move to the next answer.

How to Get Better at Smart Numbers

First, practice the problems at the end of this chapter. Try each problem two times: once using smart numbers and once using the "textbook" method. (Time yourself separately for each attempt.)

When you're done, ask yourself which way you prefer to solve *this* problem and why. On the real test, you won't have time to try both methods; you'll have to make a decision and go with it. Learn *how* to make that decision while studying; then, the next time a new problem pops up in front of you that could be solved by choosing smart numbers, you'll be able to make a quick (and good!) decision.

One important note: at first, you may find yourself always choosing the textbook approach. You've practiced algebra for years, after all, and you've only been using the smart numbers technique for a short period of time. Keep practicing; you'll get better! Every high-scorer on the Quant section will tell you that choosing smart numbers is invaluable for getting through Quant on time and with a high enough performance to reach a top score.

When NOT to Use Smart Numbers

There are certain scenarios in which a problem contains some of the smart numbers characteristics but not all.

For example, why can't you use smart numbers on this problem?

> Four brothers split a sum of money between them. The first brother received 50% of the total, the second received 25% of the total, the third received 20% of the total, and the fourth received the remaining $4. How many dollars did the four brothers split?
>
> (A) $50
> (B) $60
> (C) $75
> (D) $80
> (E) $100

The problem starts by listing percents of an unknown sum. So far, so good. Towards the end, though, it does give you one real value: $4. Because the "remaining" percent has to equal $4 exactly, this problem has just one numerical answer. You can't pick any starting point that you want. One way to tell this right away is that the answer choices are actual values rather than variable expressions or fractions or percents of an unknown whole. (The answer to the problem is (D), by the way.)

Problem Set

It's time to test out your smart numbers skills. Because recognition is a key part of using a strategy effectively, **not every question in this set can be answered using smart numbers**.

First, decide whether the problem can be answered using smart numbers. If it cannot be answered using smart numbers, answer the question algebraically. If it can, try the problem twice, once algebraically and once using smart numbers. Decide which method you prefer for each problem.

1. Bradley owns b video game cartridges. If Bradley's total is one-third the total owned by Andrew and four times the total owned by Charlie, how many video game cartridges do the three of them own altogether, in terms of b?

    (A) $\dfrac{16}{3}b$ (B) $\dfrac{17}{4}b$ (C) $\dfrac{13}{4}b$ (D) $\dfrac{19}{12}b$ (E) $\dfrac{7}{12}b$

2. Rob spends $\dfrac{1}{2}$ of his monthly paycheck, after taxes, on rent. He spends $\dfrac{1}{3}$ on food and $\dfrac{1}{8}$ on entertainment. If he donates the entire remainder, \$500, to charity, what is Rob's monthly income, after taxes?

3. Lisa spends $\dfrac{3}{8}$ of her monthly paycheck on rent and $\dfrac{5}{12}$ on food. Her roommate, Carrie, who earns twice as much as Lisa, spends $\dfrac{1}{4}$ of her monthly paycheck on rent and $\dfrac{1}{2}$ on food. If the two women decide to donate the remainder of their money to charity each month, what fraction of their combined monthly income will they donate?

6

Solutions

1. (**B**): This problem can be answered very effectively by picking numbers to represent how many video game cartridges everyone owns. Bradley owns 4 times as many cartridges as Charlie, so you should pick a value for b that is a multiple of 4.

If $b = 4$, then Charlie owns 1 cartridge and Andrew owns 12 cartridges. Together they own $4 + 1 + 12 = 17$ cartridges. Plug $b = 4$ into the answer choices and look for the one that yields 17:

$$\text{(A)}\quad \frac{16}{3}(4) = \frac{64}{3} = 21\frac{1}{3}$$

$$\text{(B)}\quad \frac{17}{4}(4) = 17 \quad \text{Match!}$$

$$\text{(C)}\quad \frac{13}{4}(4) = 13$$

$$\text{(D)}\quad \frac{19}{12}(4) = \frac{19}{3} = \text{too small to be 17}$$

$$\text{(E)}\quad \frac{7}{12}(4) = \frac{7}{3} = \text{too small to be 17}$$

The correct answer is (**B**).

2. **$12,000**: You cannot use smart numbers in this problem, because it asks you for an actual dollar amount, not a variable expression, fraction, or percent. A portion of the total is specified, so there can be only one correct amount for that total. Clearly, if you assign a number to represent the total, you will not be able to accurately find the total.

First, use addition to find the fraction of Rob's money that he spends on rent, food, and entertainment: $\frac{1}{2} + \frac{1}{3} + \frac{1}{8} = \frac{12}{24} + \frac{8}{24} + \frac{3}{24} = \frac{23}{24}$. Therefore, the $500 that he donates to charity represents $\frac{1}{24}$ of his total monthly paycheck. We can set up a proportion: $\frac{500}{x} = \frac{1}{24}$. Thus, Rob's monthly income is 500×24, or $12,000.

3. $\frac{17}{72}$: Use smart numbers to solve this problem. Since the denominators in the problem are 8, 12, 4, and 2, assign Lisa a monthly paycheck of $24. Assign her roommate, who earns twice as much, a monthly paycheck of $48. The two women's monthly expenses break down as follows:

	Rent	Food	Left over
Lisa	$\frac{3}{8}$ of 24 = 9	$\frac{5}{12}$ of 24 = 10	24 − (9 + 10) = 5
Carrie	$\frac{1}{4}$ of 48 = 12	$\frac{1}{2}$ of 48 = 24	48 − (12 + 24) = 12

The women will donate a total of $17 out of their combined monthly income of $72.

Chapter 7
of

Fractions, Decimals, & Percents

Ratios

In This Chapter...

Chapter 7
Ratios

A ratio expresses a particular relationship between two or more quantities. Here are some examples of ratios:

The ratio of men to women in the room is 3 to 4. For every 3 men, there are 4 women.

Three sisters invest in a certain stock in the ratio of 2 to 3 to 8. For every $2 the first sister invests, the second sister invests $3, and the third sister invests $8.

Two partners spend time working in the ratio of 1 to 3. For every hour the first partner works, the second partner works 3 hours.

Ratios can be expressed in three different ways:

1. Using the word *to*, as in 3 to 4
2. Using a colon, as in $3:4$ or $2:4:7$
3. By writing a fraction, as in $\dfrac{3}{4}$ (only for ratios of two quantities)

Ratios can express a part–part relationship or a part–whole relationship:

A part–part relationship: The ratio of men to women in the office is $3:4$.
A part–whole relationship: There are 3 men for every 7 employees.

Notice that if there are only two parts in the whole, you can derive a part–whole ratio from a part–part ratio, and vice versa. For example, if the ratio of men to women in the office is $3:4$, then the "total" is 7, so there are 4 women for every 7 employees.

The relationship that ratios express is division:

> If the ratio of men to women in the office is 3:4, then the number of men *divided by* the number of women equals $\frac{3}{4}$, or 0.75. In the office, there are 0.75 men for every woman.

Ratios express a *relationship* between two or more items; they do not tell you the exact quantity for each item. For example, knowing that the ratio of men to women in an office is 3 to 4 does NOT indicate the actual number of men and women in the office. There could be 3 men and 4 women, or 6 men and 8 women, or any other combination that works out to 3 men for every 4 women. Despite this, ratios are surprisingly powerful on Data Sufficiency. They often provide enough information to answer the question.

Label Each Part of the Ratio with Units

The order in which a ratio is given is vital. For example, "the ratio of dogs to cats is 2:3" is very different from "the ratio of dogs to cats is 3:2." Match the first item (dogs) to the first number (2, in the first example). Match the second item (cats) to the second number (3, in the first example).

It is very easy to accidentally reverse the order of a ratio—especially on a timed test like the GMAT. In order to avoid these reversals, write units on either the ratio itself or on the variables you create, or on both.

Thus, if the ratio of dogs to cats is 2:3, you can write $\frac{D}{C} = \frac{2\,dogs}{3\,cats}$, where D and C are variables standing for the *number* of dogs and cats (as opposed to the ratio).

The Unknown Multiplier

All ratios include something called the **unknown multiplier**. If there are 4 dogs for every 7 cats, for example, then the actual number of dogs will be a multiple of 4 and the actual number of cats will be a multiple of 7.

You can use the unknown multiplier to solve for various parts of the ratio. If the ratio of dogs to cats is 4 to 7 and there are 8 dogs total, what else can you figure out?

	Dogs	Cats	Total
Ratio	4	7	
Multiplier			
Actual	8		

The multiplier for dogs is 8/4 = 2. Here's the key: the multiplier is always the same for all parts of a ratio. Therefore, the multiplier for this entire ratio is 2:

	Dogs		**Cats**		**Total**
Ratio	4	+	7	=	
	×		×		
Multiplier	**2**	=	**2**	=	**2**
	=		=		
Actual	8	+		=	

Now, you can determine that there are 14 cats. You can also calculate the total number of animals, either by adding dogs and cats (8 + 14 = 22) or by multiplying the ratio total (4 + 7 = 11) by the multiplier, 2.

Try the below problem:

> The ratio of men to women in a room is 3 : 4. If there are 56 people in the room, how many are men?

Draw a table and begin to fill it in:

	Men	**Women**	**Total**
Ratio	3	4	
Multiplier			
Actual	○		56

You can add the top row to obtain a total of 7. The ratio of men to women to total is 3 : 4 : 7. Now you can calculate the multiplier:

	Men	**Women**	**Total**
Ratio	3	4	7
Multiplier	8	8	8
Actual	㉔		56

There are 3 × 8 = 24 men in the room.

If you prefer, you can also solve algebraically. Call the unknown multiplier x. The ratio is 3 : 4 and the actual numbers of men and women are $3x$ and $4x$, respectively.

The problem indicates that the total number of people equals 56:

$$\text{Men} + \text{Women} = \text{Total}$$
$$3x + 4x = 56$$
$$7x = 56$$
$$x = 8$$

7

Plug the multiplier into the figure for men ($3x$) to determine how many men are in the room: $(3)(8) = 24$. There are 24 men in the room.

The unknown multiplier is particularly useful with three-part ratios. For example:

> A recipe calls for amounts of lemon juice, wine, and water in the ratio of
> $2:5:7$. If all three combined yield 35 milliliters of liquid, how much wine was included?

Here's how to set it up algebraically:

$$\text{Lemon Juice} + \text{Wine} + \text{Water} = \text{Total}$$
$$2x + 5x + 7x = 14x$$

Now solve: $14x = 35$, or $x = 2.5$. Thus, the amount of wine is: $5x = 5(2.5) = 12.5$ milliliters.

In this problem, the unknown multiplier turns out not to be an integer. This result is fine, because the problem deals with continuous quantities (milliliters of liquids). In problems like the first one, which deals with integer quantities (men and women), make sure that your multiplier produces integer amounts. In that specific problem, the multiplier is literally the number of "complete sets" of 3 men and 4 women each.

Relative Values and Data Sufficiency

Some problems will give you concrete values while others will provide only relative values.

> **Concrete** values are actual amounts (# of tickets sold, liters of water, etc.).

> **Relative** values relate two quantities using fractions, decimals, percents, or ratios (twice as many, 60% less, ratio of $2:3$, etc.).

Try this problem:

> A company sells only two kinds of pie: apple pie and cherry pie. What fraction of the total pies sold last month were apple pies?
>
> (1) The company sold 460 pies last month.
> (2) The company sold 30% more cherry pies than apple pies last month.

When a question asks for a relative value, not a concrete one, you don't need as much information in order to solve.

The question asks what fraction of the total pies sold were apple pies:

$$\frac{\text{apple pies}}{\text{total pies}} = ? \quad \text{or} \quad \frac{a}{a+c} = ?$$

Statement (1) indicates that the total number of pies sold was 460, so $a + c = 460$:

$$\frac{a}{460} = ?$$

The value of a is still unknown, so this statement is not sufficient. Eliminate answer choices (A) and (D).

Statement (2) indicates that the company sold 30% more cherry pies than apple pies; in other words, the number of cherry pies sold was 130% of the number of apple pies sold:

$$1.3a = c$$

On the surface this may not seem like enough information. But watch what happens when you replace c with $1.3a$ in the rephrased question.

$$\frac{a}{a + c} = ?$$
$$\frac{a}{a + 1.3a} =$$
$$\frac{a}{2.3a} = \frac{1}{2.3}$$

Statement (2) does provide enough information to find the value of the fraction. The correct answer is **(B)**.

How could you recognize more easily that Statement (2) is sufficient?

Remember that this Data Sufficiency question was asking for a relative value (What *fraction* of the total pies…). Relative values are really just ratios in disguise. The ratio in this question is:

> apple pies sold : cherry pies sold : total pies sold

The question asks for the ratio of apple pies sold to total pies sold. Statement (2) provides the ratio of apple pies sold to cherry pies sold.

If you know any two pieces of this ratio, you can determine the third piece, so statement (2) is sufficient.

While you can determine the relative value, statement (2) does not provide enough information to calculate the actual number of pies. If the question had asked for a concrete number, such as the number of apple pies, you would have needed both statements to solve.

Multiple Ratios: Make a Common Term

You may encounter two ratios containing a common element. To combine the ratios, you can use a process remarkably similar to creating a common denominator for fractions.

Consider the following problem:

> In a box containing action figures of the three Fates from Greek mythology, there are three figures of Clotho for every two figures of Atropos, and five figures of Clotho for every four figures of Lachesis.
>
> (a) What is the least number of action figures that could be in the box?
> (b) What is the ratio of Lachesis figures to Atropos figures?

Because ratios act like fractions, you can multiply both pieces of a ratio (or all pieces, if there are more than two) by the same number, just as you can multiply the numerator and denominator of a fraction by the same number. You can change *fractions* to have common *denominators*. Likewise, you can change *ratios* to have common *terms* corresponding to the same quantity.

(a) In symbols, this problem tells you that $C:A = 3:2$ and $C:L = 5:4$. The terms for C are different (3 and 5), so you cannot immediately combine these two ratios into one. However, you can fix that problem by multiplying each ratio by the right number, turning both C's into the same number:

$$
\begin{array}{lll}
C : A : L & & C : A : L \\
3 : 2 & \rightarrow \quad \text{Multiply by 5} \quad \rightarrow & 15 : 10 \\
5 : : 4 & \rightarrow \quad \text{Multiply by 3} \quad \rightarrow & 15 : : 12 \\
& \text{This is the combined ratio:} & \boxed{15 : 10 : 12}
\end{array}
$$

Once the C's are the same (15), combine the two ratios. Note: do not add the two C's together. Just use the base number, 15.

The *actual* numbers of action figures are these three numbers multiplied by an unknown multiplier, which must be a positive integer. Using the smallest possible multiplier, 1, there are $15 + 12 + 10 = 37$ action figures.

(b) Once you have combined the ratios, you can extract the numbers corresponding to the quantities in question and disregard the others: $L:A = 12:10$, which reduces to $6:5$.

MANHATTAN
PREP

Problem Set

Solve the following problems using the strategies you have learned in this section. Use proportions and the unknown multiplier to organize ratios.

For problems 1–4, assume that neither x nor y is equal to 0, to permit division by x and by y.

1. $48:2x$ is equivalent to $144:600$. What is x?

2. $2x:y$ is equivalent to $4x:8{,}500$. What is y?

3. Initially, the men and women in a room were in the ratio of $5:7$. Six women leave the room. If there are 35 men in the room, how many women are left in the room?

4. What is the ratio $x:y:z$?

    (1) $x+y=2z$
    (2) $2x+3y=z$

Save the below problem set for review, either after you finish this book or after you finish all of the Quant books that you plan to study.

5. The amount of time that three people worked on a special project was in the ratio of 2 to 3 to 5. If the project took 110 hours, what is the difference between the number of hours worked by the person who worked for the longest time and the person who worked for the shortest time?

6. Alexandra needs to mix cleaning solution in the ratio of 1 part bleach for every 4 parts water. When mixing the solution, Alexandra makes a mistake and mixes in half as much bleach as she ought to have. The total solution consists of 27 mL. How much bleach did Alexandra put into the solution?

7

Solutions

1. **100:**

$$\frac{48}{2x} = \frac{144}{600}$$ Simplify the ratios and cancel factors horizontally across the equals sign.

$$\frac{\cancel{48}\,^{24}}{\cancel{2x}\,x} = \frac{\cancel{144}\,^{6}}{\cancel{600}\,25}$$

$$\frac{\cancel{24}\,^{4}}{x} = \frac{\cancel{6}\,^{1}}{25}$$

$$x = 100$$ Then, cross-multiply: $x = 100$.

2. **4,250:** First, simplify the ratio on the right-hand side of the equation to match the one on the left.

$$\frac{2x}{y} = \frac{\cancel{4x}\,^{2x}}{\cancel{8,500}\,^{4,250}}$$

Since the numerators are already identical, y must equal 4,250.

3. **43:** You can use the unknown multiplier very effectively here:

Men = $5x$ Women = $7x$
$5x = 35$
$x = 7$
Women = $7x = 49$

If 6 women leave the room, there are $49 - 6$, or 43, women left.

4. **(C):** For this problem, you do not necessarily need to know the value of x, y, or z. You simply need to know the ratio $x : y : z$ (in other words, the value of $\frac{x}{y}$ AND the value of $\frac{y}{z}$). You need to manipulate the information given to see whether you can determine this ratio.

(1) INSUFFICIENT: There is no way to manipulate this equation to solve for a ratio. If you simply solve for $\frac{x}{y}$, for example, you get a variable expression on the other side of the equation:

$$x + y = 2z$$
$$x = 2z - y$$
$$\frac{x}{y} = \frac{2z - y}{y} = \frac{2z}{y} - 1$$

(2) INSUFFICIENT: As in the previous example, there is no way to manipulate this equation to solve for $\frac{x}{y}$, for example, you get a variable expression on the other side of the equation:

$$2x + 3y = z$$

$$2x = z - 3y$$

$$\frac{x}{y} = \frac{z - 3y}{2y} = \frac{z}{2y} - \frac{3}{2}$$

(1) AND (2) SUFFICIENT: Use substitution to combine the equations:

$$x + y = 2z$$

$$2x + 3y = z$$

Since $z = 2x + 3y$, you can substitute:

$$x + y = 2(2x + 3y)$$

$$x + y = 4x + 6y$$

Therefore, you can arrive at a value for the ratio $x : y$:

$$-3x = 5y$$

$$\frac{-3x}{y} = \frac{5\cancel{y}}{\cancel{y}} \qquad \text{Divide by } y.$$

$$\frac{\cancel{-3}x}{\cancel{-3}y} = \frac{5}{-3} \qquad \text{Divide by } -3.$$

$$\frac{x}{y} = \frac{5}{-3}$$

You can also substitute for x to get a value for the ratio $y : z$:

$$x + y = 2z$$

$$x = 2z - y$$

$$2x + 3y = z$$

$$2(2z - y) + 3y = z$$

$$4z - 2y + 3y = z$$

$$y = -3z$$

$$\frac{y}{z} = -3$$

MANHATTAN
PREP

This tells you that $x:y = -5/3$, and $y:z = -3/1$. Both ratios contain a 3 for the y variable and both also contain a negative sign, so assign the value -3 to y. This means that x must be 5 and z must be 1. Therefore, the ratio $x:y:z = 5:-3:1$.

You can test the result by choosing $x = 5$, $y = -3$, and $z = 1$, or $x = 10$, $y = -6$, and $z = 2$. In either case, the original equations hold up.

The correct answer is **(C)**.

5. **33 hours:** Use an equation with the unknown multiplier to represent the total hours put in by the three people:

$$2x + 3x + 5x = 110$$
$$10x = 110$$
$$x = 11$$

Therefore, the person who worked for the longest time put in $5(11) = 55$ hours, and the person who worked for the shortest time put in $2(11) = 22$ hours. This represents a difference of $55 - 22 = 33$ hours.

6. **3 mL:** The correct ratio is $1:4$, which means that there should be x parts bleach and $4x$ parts water. However, Alexandra put in half as much bleach as she should have, so she put in $\dfrac{x}{2}$ parts bleach. You can represent this with an equation: $\dfrac{x}{2} + 4x = 27$. Now solve for x:

$$x + 8x = 54$$
$$9x = 54$$
$$x = 6$$

You were asked to find how much bleach Alexandra used. This equaled $\dfrac{x}{2}$, so Alexandra used $\dfrac{6}{2} = 3$ mL of bleach.

7

Chapter 8

of

Fractions, Decimals, & Percents

Strategy: Estimation

In This Chapter...

Chapter 8

Strategy: Estimation

You can estimate your way to an answer on problems with certain characteristics. Try these two problems:

1. $\dfrac{7}{13}+\dfrac{5}{11}$ is approximately equal to

   (A) 0   (B) 1   (C) 2

2. Of 450 employees at a company, 20% are managers and the rest are not managers. If 60% of the managers work in the engineering department, how many managers do not work in the engineering department?

   (A) 36   (B) 54   (C) 90

Before you look at the solutions in the next section, try to figure out how you would know that you can estimate on these two problems.

How to Estimate

The first problem actually tells you that you can estimate. Whenever a problem contains the word approximately (or an equivalent word), do not even try to do exact calculations. Take the problem at its word and estimate!

1. $\dfrac{7}{13}+\dfrac{5}{11}$ is approximately equal to

   (A) 0   (B) 1   (C) 2

Converting to common denominators here would be pretty annoying, as would converting the fractions to decimals or percents. Instead, round those fractions to easier ones and find an approximate answer.

$\dfrac{7}{13}$ is very close to $\dfrac{7}{14}$, or $\dfrac{1}{2}$, so call that first fraction 0.5.

Note that $\frac{7}{13}$ is a little larger than $\frac{7}{14}$; in other words, you rounded down. Try to offset the error by rounding in the other direction (up) next time.

Since $\frac{5}{11}$ is a little bit less than $\frac{1}{2}$, you can round up this time. Call the second fraction 0.5 as well.

In this case, then, $0.5 + 0.5 = 1$, so the answer is **(B)**.

The second problem doesn't tell you that you can estimate; nevertheless, it contains an important clue that points towards estimation.

Remember this graphic from Chapter 1?

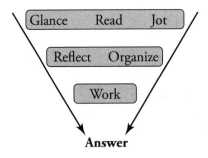

On all Problem Solving problems, get in the habit of glancing at the answers during your first step (Glance, Read, Jot). Whenever the answers are far apart, you can estimate. (Note that the numbers only need to be far apart in relative terms—in the last problem, the numbers are only 1 apart, but 2 is twice as big as 1, and there's a big difference between 1 and 0.)

2. Of 450 employees at a company, 20% are managers and the rest are not managers. If 60% of the managers work in the engineering department, how many managers do not work in the engineering department?

    (A) 36   (B) 54   (C) 90

The three answers are pretty far apart, so plan to estimate wherever it makes sense in the process.

The question asks for the number of managers who do not work in engineering. First, find the number of managers, which is 20% of 450: 10% of 450 is 45, so 20% is twice as much, or 90.

There are 90 managers total, so (C) cannot be the answer; cross it off. (If there were larger answers, you could of course cross those off, too.) Further, if 60% of those managers work in engineering, then 40% (or less than half) do not. Half of 90 is 45, so the number of managers not in engineering must be less than 45. The only possible answer is **(A)**.

When to Estimate

Estimate whenever the problem explicitly asks for an approximate answer. In addition, consider estimating when the answers are far apart or when they cover certain "divided" characteristics.

In some cases, this estimation will get you all the way to the correct answer. In others, you may be able to eliminate some answers before guessing on a hard problem.

Consider these possible answers:

(A) −6   (B) −3   (C) −2   (D) 1   (E) 2

If you are running out of time or are not sure how to answer the question in the normal way, you may at least be able to tell whether the answer should be positive or negative. If so, you'll be able to eliminate two or three answers before making a guess.

A fraction problem might have some answers greater than 1 and others less than 1. You may also be able to estimate here in order to eliminate some answers.

Benchmark Values

Benchmark values are common percents or fractions that make estimation easier. The easiest percent benchmarks are 50%, 10%, and 1%. The easiest fraction benchmarks are $\frac{1}{2}$, the quarters $\left(\frac{1}{4}, \frac{3}{4}\right)$, and the thirds $\left(\frac{1}{3}, \frac{2}{3}\right)$.

You may be able to use the building percents calculation method, first introduced in chapter 5, to estimate.

Try this problem:

> When Karen bought a new television, originally priced at $700, she used a coupon for a 12% discount. What price did she pay for the television?
>
> (A) $630   (B) $616   (C) $560

Because 10% of 700 is 70, you know Karen received something more than a $70 discount. She must have paid a bit less than $630. Answer (A) can't be correct.

A 20% discount would have resulted in another $70 off, for a total $140 discount, or $560. Answer (C) is too small. The correct answer must be **(B)**.

8

(Indeed, if you check the math, 10% + 1% + 1% = 70 + 7 + 7 = $84, and 700 − 84 = $616. But don't do this math on the test unless it's necessary!)

You can also use benchmark values to compare fractions:

$$\text{Which is greater: } \frac{127}{255} \text{ or } \frac{162}{320}?$$

How does each fraction compare to $\frac{1}{2}$? It turns out that 127 is less than half of 255 and 162 is more than half of 320, so $\frac{162}{320}$ is the greater fraction.

You can also use benchmark values to estimate computations involving fractions:

$$\text{What is } \frac{10}{22} \text{ of } \frac{5}{18} \text{ of 2,000?}$$

Once you determine that $\frac{10}{22}$ is a little bit less than $\frac{1}{2}$ and $\frac{5}{18}$ is a little bit more than $\frac{1}{4}$, you can use these benchmarks to estimate:

$$\frac{1}{2} \text{ of } \frac{1}{4} \text{ of 2,000} = 250$$

Therefore, $\frac{10}{22}$ of $\frac{5}{18}$ of 2,000 ≈ 250.

Notice that the rounding errors compensated for each other:

$$\frac{10}{22} \approx \frac{10}{20} = \frac{1}{2} \qquad \text{You decreased the denominator, so you rounded up: } \frac{10}{22} < \frac{1}{2}.$$

$$\frac{5}{18} \approx \frac{5}{20} = \frac{1}{4} \qquad \text{You increased the denominator, so you rounded down: } \frac{5}{18} > \frac{1}{4}.$$

If you had rounded $\frac{5}{18}$ to $\frac{6}{18} = \frac{1}{3}$ instead, then you would have rounded both fractions up. This would lead to a slight but systematic overestimation:

$$\frac{1}{2} \times \frac{1}{3} \times 2{,}000 \approx 333$$

Try to make your rounding errors cancel by rounding some numbers up and others down.

8

How to Get Better at Estimation

First, try the problems associated with this chapter in your online *Official Guide* problem sets. Try doing the official math *and* estimating to see how much time and effort estimation can save you.

If you have to estimate more than once in a problem, try to round up once and down once in order to minimize the rounding errors.

If you have trouble with any part of the process, try the problem again, making sure to write out all of your work.

Afterwards, use your notes to think your way through the problem again. How did you know you could estimate? At which point in the problem did the estimation come into play? Could you have streamlined the process or made better estimates at any step along the way?

If you struggle with any of this, look up the solution in GMAT Navigator™, consult the Manhattan Prep forums, or ask an instructor or fellow student for help.

Chapter *of* 9

Fractions, Decimals, & Percents

Extra FDPs

In This Chapter...

Chapter 9
Extra FDPs

This chapter outlines miscellaneous extra topics within the areas of *fractions, decimals, percents, and ratios*. If you have mastered the material in earlier chapters and are aiming for an especially high Quant score, then learn this material. If not, then you may be able to skip this section.

Exponents and Roots

To square or cube a decimal, you can always multiply it by itself once or twice. However, to raise a decimal to a higher power, you can rewrite the decimal as the product of an integer and a power of 10, and then apply the exponent:

$(0.5)^4 = ?$

$0.5 = 5 \times 10^{-1}$	Rewrite the decimal.
$(5 \times 10^{-1})^4 = 5^4 \times 10^{-4}$	Apply the exponent to each part.
$5^4 = 25^2 = 625$	Compute the first part and combine.
$625 \times 10^{-4} = 0.0625$	

Solve for roots of decimals the same way. Recall that a root is a number raised to a fractional power: a square root is a number raised to the 1/2 power, a cube root is a number raised to the 1/3 power, etc.:

$\sqrt[3]{0.000027} = ?$

Rewrite the decimal. Make the first number something you can take the cube root of easily:

$0.000027 = 27 \times 10^{-6}$

$(0.000027)^{1/3} = (27 \times 10^{-6})^{1/3}$	Write the root as a fractional exponent.
$(27)^{1/3} \times (10^{-6})^{1/3} = (27)^{1/3} \times 10^{-2}$	Apply the exponent to each part.
$(27)^{1/3} = 3 \qquad$ (since $3^3 = 27$)	Compute the first part and combine.
$3 \times 10^{-2} = 0.03$	

Strategy Tip: Powers and roots: Rewrite the decimal using powers of 10!

Once you understand the principles, you can take a shortcut by counting decimal places. For instance, the number of decimal places in a cubed decimal is 3 times the number of decimal places in the original decimal:

$$(0.04)^3 = 0.000064 \qquad\qquad (0.04)^3 \qquad\qquad = 0.000064$$
$$2\ places \qquad\qquad 2 \times 3 = 6\ places$$

Likewise, the number of decimal places in a cube root is 1/3 the number of decimal places in the original decimal:

$$\sqrt[3]{0.000000008} = 0.002 \qquad \sqrt[3]{0.000000008} \qquad = 0.002$$
$$9\ places \qquad\qquad 9 \div 3 = 3\ places$$

Repeating Decimals

Dividing an integer by another integer yields a decimal that either terminates or never ends and repeats itself:

$$2 \div 9 = ? \qquad 9\overline{)2.000} \qquad 2 \div 9 = 0.2222\ldots = 0.\overline{2}$$

Generally, do long division to determine the repeating cycle. However, you can use any patterns you've memorized to reduce your workload. For instance, if you've memorized that 1/9 is $0.\overline{1}$, you can determine that 2/9 is $0.\overline{2}$.

It can also be helpful to know that if the denominator is 9, 99, 999 or another number equal to a power of 10 minus 1, then the numerator tells you the repeating digits. Here are two examples:

$$23 \div 99 = 0.2323\ldots = 0.\overline{23} \qquad \frac{3}{11} = \frac{27}{99} = 0.2727\ldots = 0.\overline{27}$$

Terminating Decimals

Some numbers, like $\sqrt{2}$ and π, have decimals that never end and *never* repeat themselves. On certain problems, it can be useful to use approximations for these decimals (e.g., $\sqrt{2} \approx 1.4$). Occasionally, though, the GMAT asks you about properties of "terminating" decimals; that is, decimals that end. You can tack on zeroes, of course, but they don't matter. Some examples of terminating decimals are 0.2, 0.47, and 0.375.

Terminating decimals can all be written as a ratio of integers (which might be reducible):

$$\frac{\text{Some integer}}{\text{Some power of 10}}$$

$$0.2 = \frac{2}{10} = \frac{1}{5} \qquad 0.47 = \frac{47}{100} \qquad 0.375 = \frac{375}{1,000} = \frac{3}{8}$$

Positive powers of 10 are composed of only 2's and 5's as prime factors. When you reduce this fraction, you only have prime factors of 2's and/or 5's in the denominator. Every terminating decimal shares this characteristic. If, after being fully reduced, the denominator has any prime factors besides 2 or 5, then its decimal will not terminate. If the denominator only has factors of 2 and/or 5, then the decimal will terminate.

Using Place Value on the GMAT

Some difficult GMAT problems require the use of place value with unknown digits. For example:

> A and B are both two-digit numbers, and A > B. If A and B contain the same digits, but in reverse order, what integer must be a factor of (A − B)?
>
> (A) 4   (B) 5   (C) 6   (D) 8   (E) 9

To solve this problem, assign two variables to be the digits in A and B: x and y. Let $A = \boxed{x}\boxed{y}$ (**not** the product of x and y: x is in the tens place, and y is in the units place). The boxes remind you that x and y stand for digits. A is therefore the sum of x tens and y ones. Using algebra, write $A = 10x + y$.

Since B's digits are reversed, $B = \boxed{y}\boxed{x}$. Algebraically, B can be expressed as $10y + x$. The difference of A and B can be expressed as follows:

$$A - B = 10x + y - (10y + x) = 9x - 9y = 9(x - y)$$

Therefore, 9 must be a factor of $A - B$. The correct answer is **(E)**.

You can also make up digits for x and y and plug them in to create A and B. This will not necessarily yield the unique right answer, but it will help you eliminate wrong choices.

In general, for unknown digits problems, be ready to create variables (such as x, y, and z) to represent the unknown digits. Recognize that each unknown is restricted to at most 10 possible values (0 through 9). Then apply any given constraints, which may involve number properties such as divisibility or odds and evens.

9

The Last Digit Shortcut

Sometimes the GMAT asks you to find a units digit, or a remainder after division by 10:

What is the units digit of $(7)^2(9)^2(3)^3$?

In this problem, you can use the **last digit shortcut**:

To find the units digit of a product or a sum of integers, only pay attention to the units digits of the numbers you are working with. Drop any other digits.

This shortcut works because only units digits contribute to the units digit of the product:

Step 1:	$7 \times 7 = 49$	Drop the tens digit and keep only the last digit: 9.
Step 2:	$9 \times 9 = 81$	Drop the tens digit and keep only the last digit: 1.
Step 3:	$3 \times 3 \times 3 = 27$	Drop the tens digit and keep only the last digit: 7.
Step 4:	$9 \times 1 \times 7 = 63$	Multiply the last digits of each of the products.

The units digit of the final product is 3.

Unknown Digits Problems

Occasionally, the GMAT asks tough problems involving unknown digits. These problems look like "brainteasers"; it seems it could take all day to test the possible digits.

However, like all other GMAT problems, these digit "brainteasers" must be solvable under time constraints. As a result, there are always ways of reducing the number of possibilities:

Principles:

- Look at the answer choices first, to limit your search.
- Use other given constraints to rule out additional possibilities.
- Focus on the units digit in the product or sum. This units digit is affected by the fewest other digits.
- Test the remaining answer choices.

9

Example:

$$\begin{array}{r} AB \\ \times\ CA \\ \hline DEBC \end{array}$$

In the multiplication above, each letter stands for a different non-zero digit, with A × B < 10. What is the two-digit number AB?

(A) 23   (B) 24   (C) 25   (D) 32   (E) 42

It is often helpful to look at the answer choices. Here, you see that the possible digits for A and B are 2, 3, 4, and 5.

Next, apply the given constraint that A × B < 10. This rules out answer choice (C), 25, since 2 × 5 = 10.

Now, test the remaining answer choices. Notice that A × B = C, the units digit of the product. Therefore, you can find all the needed digits and complete each multiplication.

Compare each result to the template. The two positions of the B digit must match (note that it's not really necessary to calculate past the tens digit):

$$\begin{array}{r} 23 \\ \times\ 62 \\ \hline 1,426 \end{array} \qquad\qquad \begin{array}{r} 24 \\ \times\ 82 \\ \hline 1,968 \end{array}$$

The B's do not match   The B's do not match

$$\begin{array}{r} 32 \\ \times\ 63 \\ \hline 2,016 \end{array} \qquad\qquad \begin{array}{r} 42 \\ \times\ 84 \\ \hline 3,528 \end{array}$$

The B's do not match   The B's match

The correct answer is **(E)**.

Note that you could have used the constraints to derive the possible digits (2, 3, and 4) without using the answer choices. However, for these problems, take advantage of the answer choices to restrict your search quickly.

9

Problem Set

1. What is the units digit of $\left(\dfrac{6^6}{6^5}\right)^6$?

2. What is the units digit of $(2)^5(3)^3(4)^2$?

3. Order from least to greatest:

    $\dfrac{\frac{3}{5}}{\frac{8}{10}}$ $\dfrac{0.00751}{0.01}$ $\dfrac{200}{3}\times10^{-2}$

4. What is the length of the sequence of different digits in the decimal equivalent of $\dfrac{3}{7}$?

5. Which of the following fractions will terminate when expressed as a decimal? (Choose all that apply.)

    (A) $\dfrac{1}{256}$ (B) $\dfrac{27}{100}$ (C) $\dfrac{100}{27}$ (D) $\dfrac{231}{660}$ (E) $\dfrac{7}{105}$

6. The number A is a two-digit positive integer; the number B is the two-digit positive integer formed by reversing the digits of A. If $Q = 10B - A$, what is the value of Q?

    (1) The tens digit of A is 7.
    (2) The tens digit of B is 6.

7.

    In the multiplication above, each symbol represents a different unknown digit, and
    ● × ■ × ◆ = 36. What is the three-digit integer ●■◆?

    (A) 263   (B) 236   (C) 194   (D) 491   (E) 452

9

Solutions

1. **6:** First, use the rules for combining exponents to simplify the expression. Subtract the exponents to get $\frac{6^6}{6^5} = 6^1$. Then, raise this to the sixth power: $(6^1)^6 = 6^6$. Ignore any digits other than the units digit. No matter how many times you multiply 6×6, the result will still end in 6. The units digit is 6.

2. **4:** Use the last digit shortcut, ignoring all digits but the last in any intermediate products:

    Step 1: $2^5 = 32$ Drop the tens digit and keep only the last digit: 2.

    Step 2: $3^3 = 27$ Drop the tens digit and keep only the last digit: 7.

    Step 3: $4^2 = 16$ Drop the tens digit and keep only the last digit: 6.

    Step 4: $2 \times 7 \times 6 = 84$ Multiply the last digits of each of the products and keep only the last digit: 4.

3. $\dfrac{200}{3} \times 10^{-2} < \dfrac{3}{5} \div \dfrac{8}{10} < \dfrac{0.00751}{0.01}$

First, simplify all terms and express them in decimal form:

$$\frac{3}{5} \div \frac{8}{10} = \frac{3}{5} \times \frac{10}{8} = \frac{3}{4} = 0.75$$

$$\frac{0.00751}{0.01} = \frac{0.751}{1} = 0.751$$

$$\frac{200}{3} \times 10^{-2} = \frac{2}{3} = 0.\overline{6}$$

$$0.\overline{6} < 0.75 < 0.751$$

4. **6:** Generally, the easiest way to find the pattern of digits in a non-terminating decimal is to simply do the long division and wait for the pattern to repeat (see long division at right). This results in a repeating pattern of $0.\overline{428571}$.

```
        0.4285714
    7)3.0000000
       0
      ───
      3.0
      2.8
      ───
       20
      -14
      ────
        60
      - 56
      ────
        40
      - 35
      ────
        50
      - 49
      ────
        10
       - 7
      ────
        30
      - 28
      ────
         2
```

5. **(A), (B), and (D):** Recall that in order for the decimal version of a fraction to terminate, the fraction's denominator in fully reduced form must have a prime factorization that consists of only 2's and/or 5's. The denominator in (A) is composed of only 2's ($256 = 2^8$). The denominator in (B) is composed of only 2's and 5's ($100 = 2^2 \times 5^2$).

In fully reduced form, the fraction in (D) is equal to $\dfrac{7}{20}$, and 20 is composed of only 2's and 5's ($20 = 2^2 \times 5$). By contrast, the denominator in (C) has prime factors other than 2's and 5's ($27 = 3^3$), and in fully reduced form, the fraction in (E) is equal to $\dfrac{1}{15}$, and 15 has a prime factor other than 2's and 5's ($15 = 3 \times 5$).

6. **(B):** Write A as XY, where X and Y are digits (X is the tens digit of A and Y is the units digit of A). Then B can be written as YX, with reversed digits. Writing these numbers in algebraic rather than digital form, you have $A = 10X + Y$ and $B = 10Y + X$.

9

Therefore, $Q = 10B - A = 10(10Y + X) - (10X + Y) = 100Y + 10X - 10X - Y = 99Y$. The value of Q only depends on the value of Y, which is the tens digit of B. The value of X is irrelevant to Q. Therefore, statement (2) alone is SUFFICIENT.

You can also test cases to get the same result, although algebra is probably faster if you are comfortable with the setup. To test cases here, you'd need to try different two-digit numbers that fit the constraints for each statement:

(1) INSUFFICIENT:

$$A = 72, B = 27, 10B - A = 198$$
$$A = 73, B = 37, 10B - A = 297$$

(2) SUFFICIENT:

$$A = 26, B = 62, 10B - A = 594$$
$$A = 76, B = 67, 10B - A = 594$$

Without the benefit of algebra, it may not be clear why statement (2) always produces the same answer, but if you get the exact same number from two different values on a problem with such involved math, chances are good that a consistent pattern is emerging.

7. **(B):** The three symbols ●, ■, and ◆ multiply to 36 and each must represent a different digit. Take a look at those answer choices: you can work backwards to solve! The digits of each answer choice represent ●, ■, ◆, respectively. Plug each in to find the one that works.

(A) 263. The multiplication problem becomes (23)(63). The units digit is 9, but it should be 3, so this answer is incorrect.

(B) 236. The multiplication problem becomes (26)(36). The units digit is 6, so this one could work. At this point, decide whether you want to finish the rest of the math for this answer or whether you want to check for the units digit for (C), (D), and (E). If the units digit doesn't work for the other three, then this one must be the right answer and you don't have to do any more work.

Here's the rest of the work for (B). (26)(36) = 936. This does match the remaining restrictions on the problem, so it is the correct answer.

(C) 194. The multiplication problem becomes (14)(94). The units digit is 6, but it should be 4, so this answer is incorrect.

(D) 491. The multiplication problem becomes (41)(91). The units digit is 1, so you also have more work to do on this choice. (41)(91) = 3,731. The product has to be a 3-digit number, not a 4-digit number, so this answer is incorrect. (You can stop the multiplication at the point that you can tell that it will be larger than a 3-digit number.)

(E) 452. These three digits don't multiply to 36, so this cannot be the correct answer.

Appendix A

of

Fractions, Decimals, & Percents

Data Sufficiency

In This Chapter...

Appendix A
Data Sufficiency

Data Sufficiency (DS) problems are a cross between math and logic. Imagine that your boss just walked into your office and dumped a bunch of papers on your desk, saying, "Hey, our client wants to know whether they should raise the price on this product. Can you answer that question from this data? If so, which pieces do we need to prove the case?" What would you do?

The client has asked a specific question: should the company raise the price? You have to decide which pieces of information will allow you to answer that question—or, possibly, that you don't have enough information to answer the question at all.

This kind of logical reasoning is exactly what you use when you answer DS questions.

How Data Sufficiency Works

If you already feel comfortable with the basics of Data Sufficiency, you may want to move quickly through this particular section of the chapter—but you are encouraged to read it. There are a few insights that you may find useful.

Every DS problem has the same basic form:

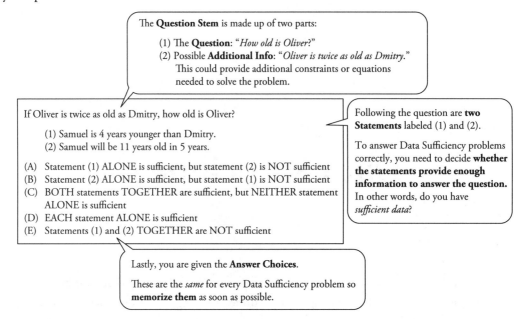

The **Question Stem** is made up of two parts:

(1) The **Question**: "*How old is Oliver?*"
(2) Possible **Additional Info**: "*Oliver is twice as old as Dmitry.*"
    This could provide additional constraints or equations needed to solve the problem.

If Oliver is twice as old as Dmitry, how old is Oliver?

(1) Samuel is 4 years younger than Dmitry.
(2) Samuel will be 11 years old in 5 years.

(A) Statement (1) ALONE is sufficient, but statement (2) is NOT sufficient
(B) Statement (2) ALONE is sufficient, but statement (1) is NOT sufficient
(C) BOTH statements TOGETHER are sufficient, but NEITHER statement ALONE is sufficient
(D) EACH statement ALONE is sufficient
(E) Statements (1) and (2) TOGETHER are NOT sufficient

Following the question are **two Statements** labeled (1) and (2).

To answer Data Sufficiency problems correctly, you need to decide **whether the statements provide enough information to answer the question.** In other words, do you have *sufficient data*?

Lastly, you are given the **Answer Choices**.

These are the *same* for every Data Sufficiency problem so **memorize them** as soon as possible.

The question stem contains the question you need to answer. The two statements provide *given* information, information that is true. DS questions look strange but you can think of them as deconstructed Problem Solving (PS) questions. Compare the DS-format problem above to the PS-format problem below:

> Samuel is 4 years younger than Dmitry, and Samuel will be 11 years old in 5 years.
> If Oliver is twice as old as Dmitry, how old is Oliver?"

The two questions contain exactly the same information; that information is just presented in a different order. The PS question stem contains all of the givens as well as the question. The DS problem moves some of the givens down to statement (1) and statement (2).

As with regular PS problems, the given information in the DS statements is always true. In addition, the two statements won't contradict each other. In the same way that a PS question wouldn't tell you that $x > 0$ *and* $x < 0$, the two DS statements won't do that either.

In the PS format, you would go ahead and calculate Oliver's age. The DS format works a bit differently. Here is the full problem, including the answer choices:

> If Oliver is twice as old as Dmitry, how old is Oliver?
>
> (1) Samuel is 4 years younger than Dmitry.
> (2) Samuel will be 11 years old in 5 years.
>
> (A) Statement (1) ALONE is sufficient, but statement (2) is NOT sufficient.
> (B) Statement (2) ALONE is sufficient, but statement (1) is NOT sufficient.
> (C) BOTH statements TOGETHER are sufficient, but NEITHER statement ALONE is sufficient.
> (D) EACH statement ALONE is sufficient.
> (E) Statements (1) and (2) TOGETHER are NOT sufficient.

Despite all appearances, the question is not actually asking you to calculate Oliver's age. Rather, it's asking *which pieces of information* would allow you to calculate Oliver's age.

You may already be able solve this one on your own, but you'll see much harder problems on the test, so your first task is to learn how to work through DS questions in a systematic, consistent way.

As you think the problem through, jot down information from the question stem:

$$O\ age = \underline{\quad} ?$$
$$O = 2D$$

Hmm. If they tell you Dmitry's age, then you can find Oliver's age. Remember that!

Take a look at the first statement. Also, write down the $\frac{AD}{BCE}$ answer grid (you'll learn why as you work through the problem):

(1) Samuel is 4 years younger than Dmitry.

$$O\ age = \underline{\quad} ? \qquad AD$$
$$O = 2D \qquad\qquad BCE$$
$$(1)\ S = D - 4 \quad | \quad (2)$$

The first statement doesn't allow you to figure out anyone's real age. Statement (1), then, is *not sufficient*. Now you can cross off the top row of answers, (A) and (D).

Why? Here's the text for answers (A) and (D):

  (A) Statement (1) ALONE is sufficient, but statement (2) is NOT sufficient.
  (D) EACH statement ALONE is sufficient.

Both answers indicate that statement (1) is sufficient to answer the question. Because statement (1) is *not* sufficient to find Oliver's age, both (A) and (D) are wrong.

The answer choices will always appear in the order shown for the above problem, so any time you decide that statement (1) is not sufficient, you will always cross off answers (A) and (D). That's why your answer grid groups these two answers together.

Next, consider statement (2), but remember one tricky thing: forget what statement (1) told you. Because of the way DS is constructed, you must evaluate the two statements separately before you look at them together:

(2) Samuel will be 11 years old in 5 years.

It's useful to write the two statements side-by-side, as shown above, to help remember that statement (2) is separate from statement (1) and has to be considered by itself first.

Statement (2) does indicate how old Sam is now, but says nothing about Oliver or Dmitry. (Remember, you're looking *only* at statement (2) now.) By itself, statement (2) is not sufficient, so cross off answer (B).

Now that you've evaluated each statement by itself, take a look at the two statements together. Statement (2) provides Sam's age, and statement (1) allows you to calculate Dmitry's age if you know Sam's age. Finally, the question stem allows you to calculate Oliver's age if you know Dmitry's age:

As soon as you can tell that you *can* solve, put down a check mark or write an S with a circle around it (or both!). Don't actually calculate Oliver's age; the GMAT doesn't give you any extra time to calculate a number that you don't need.

The correct answer is (C).

The Answer Choices

The five Data Sufficiency answer choices will always be exactly the same (and presented in the same order), so memorize them before you go into the test.

Here are the five answers written in an easier way to understand:

> (A) Statement (1) does allow you to answer the question, but statement (2) does not.
> (B) Statement (2) does allow you to answer the question, but statement (1) does not.
> (C) Neither statement works on its own, but you can use them *together* to answer the question.
> (D) Statement (1) works by itself *and* statement (2) works by itself.
> (E) Nothing works. Even if you use both statements together, you still can't answer the question.

Answer (C) specifically says that neither statement works on its own. For this reason, you are required to look at each statement by itself *and decide that neither one works* before you are allowed to evaluate the two statements together.

Here's an easier way to remember the five answer choices; we call this the "twelve-ten" mnemonic (memory aid):

1	only statement 1
2	only statement 2
T	together
E	either one
N	neither/nothing

Within the next week, memorize the DS answers. If you do a certain number of practice DS problems in that time frame, you'll likely memorize the answers without conscious effort—and you'll solidify the DS lessons you're learning right now.

Starting with Statement (2)

If statement (1) looks hard, start with statement (2) instead. Your process will be the same, except you'll make one change in your answer grid.

Try this problem:

> If Oliver is twice as old as Dmitry, how old is Oliver?
>
> (1) Two years ago, Dmitry was twice as old as Samuel.
> (2) Samuel is 6 years old.

(From now on, the answer choices won't be shown. Start memorizing!)

Statement (1) is definitely more complicated than statement (2), so start with statement (2) instead. Change your answer grid to $\frac{\text{BD}}{\text{ACE}}$. (You'll learn why in a minute.)

(2) Samuel is 6 years old.

Statement (2) is not sufficient to determine Oliver's age, so cross off the answers that say statement (2) is sufficient: (B) and (D). Once again, you can cross off the entire top row; when starting with statement (2), you always will keep or eliminate these two choices at the same time.

Now assess statement (1):

(1) Two years ago, Dmitry was twice as old as Samuel.

Forget all about statement (2); only statement (1) exists. By itself, is the statement sufficient?

Nope! Too many variables. Cross off (A), the first of the remaining answers in the bottom row, and assess the two statements together:

You can plug Samuel's age (from the second statement) into the formula from statement (1) to find Dmitry's age, and then use Dmitry's age to find Oliver's age. Together, the statements are sufficient.

The correct answer is **(C)**.

The two answer grids work in the same way, regardless of which one you use. As long as you use the AD/BCE grid when starting with statement (1), or the BD/ACE grid when starting with statement (2), you will always:

- cross off the *top* row if the first statement you try is *not* sufficient;
- cross off the *bottom* row if the first statement you try *is* sufficient; and
- assess the remaining row of answers one answer at a time.

Finally, remember that you must assess the statements separately before you can try them together—and you'll only try them together if neither one is sufficient on its own. You will only consider the two together if you have already crossed off answers (A), (B), and (D).

Value vs. Yes/No Questions

Data Sufficiency questions come in two "flavors": Value or Yes/No.

On Value questions, it is necessary to find a single value in order to answer the question. If you can't find any value or you can find two or more values, then the information is not sufficient.

Consider this statement:

(1) Oliver's age is a multiple of 4.

Oliver could be 4 or 8 or 12 or any age that is a multiple of 4. Because it's impossible to determine one particular value for Oliver's age, the statement is not sufficient

What if the question changed?

Is Oliver's age an even number?

(1) Oliver's age is a multiple of 4.
(2) Oliver is between 19 and 23 years old.

This question is a Yes/No question. There are three possible answers to a Yes/No question:

1. Always Yes: Sufficient!
2. Always No: Sufficient!
3. Maybe (or Sometimes Yes, Sometimes No): Not Sufficient

It may surprise you that Always No is sufficient to answer the question. Imagine that you ask a friend to go to the movies with you. If she says, "No, I'm sorry, I can't," then you did receive an answer to your question (even though the answer is negative). You know she can't go to the movies with you.

Apply this reasoning to the Oliver question. Is statement 1 sufficient to answer the question *Is Oliver's age an even number?*

> (1) Oliver's age is a multiple of 4.

If Oliver's age is a multiple of 4, then Yes, he must be an even number of years old. The information isn't enough to tell how old Oliver actually is—he could be 4, 8, 12, or any multiple of 4 years old. Still, the information is sufficient to answer the specific question asked.

Because the statement tried first is sufficient, cross off the bottom row of answers, (B), (C), and (E).

Next, check statement (2):

> (2) Oliver is between 19 and 23 years old.

Oliver could be 20, in which case his age is even. He could also be 21, in which case his age is odd. The answer here is Sometimes Yes, Sometimes No, so the information is not sufficient to answer the question.

The correct answer is **(A)**: the first statement is sufficient but the second is not.

The DS Process

This section summarizes everything you've learned in one consistent DS process. You can use this on every DS problem on the test.

Step 1: Determine whether the question is Value or Yes/No.

Value: The question asks for the value of an unknown (e.g., What is x?).

A statement is **Sufficient** when it provides **1 possible value**.

A statement is **Not Sufficient** when it provides **more than 1 possible value** (or none at all).

Yes/No: The question asks whether a given piece of information is true (e.g., Is x even?). Most of the time, these will be in the form of Yes/No questions.

A statement is **Sufficient** when the answer is **Always Yes** or **Always No**.

A statement is **Not Sufficient** when the answer is **Maybe** or **Sometimes Yes, Sometimes No**.

Step 2: Separate given information from the question itself.

If the question stem contains given information—that is, any information other than the question itself—then write down that information separately from the question itself. This is true information that you must consider or use when answering the question.

Step 3: Rephrase the question.

Most of the time, you will not write down the entire question stem exactly as it appears on screen. At the least, you'll simplify what is written on screen. For example, if the question stem asks, "What is the value of x?" then you might write down something like $x =$ _____ ?

For more complicated question stems, you may have more work to do. Ideally, before you go to the statements, you will be able to articulate a fairly clear and straightforward question. In the earlier example, $x =$ _____ ? is clear and straightforward.

What if this is the question?

> If $xyz \neq 0$, is $\dfrac{3x}{2} + y + 2z = \dfrac{7x}{2} + y$?
>
> (1) $y = 3$ and $x = 2$
> (2) $z = -x$

Do you need to know the individual values of x, y, and z in order to answer the question? Would knowing the value of a combination of the variables, such as $x + y + z$, work? It's tough to tell.

In order to figure this out, ***rephrase*** the question stem, which is a fancy way of saying: simplify the information a lot. Take the time to do this before you address the statements; you'll make your job much easier!

If you're given an equation, the first task is to put the "like" variables together. Also, when working with the question stem, make sure to carry the question mark through your work:

$$y - y + 2z = \dfrac{7x}{2} - \dfrac{3x}{2}?$$

That's interesting: the two y variables cancel out. Keep simplifying:

$$2z = \dfrac{4x}{2}?$$
$$2z = 2x?$$
$$z = x?$$

That whole crazy equation is really asking a much simpler question: is $z = x$?

It might seem silly to keep writing that question mark at the end of each line, but don't skip that step or you'll be opening yourself up to a careless error. By the time you get to the end, you don't want to forget that this is still a *question*, not a statement or given.

Step 4: Use the Answer Grid to Evaluate the Statements

If you start with statement 1, then write the AD/BCE grid on your scrap paper.

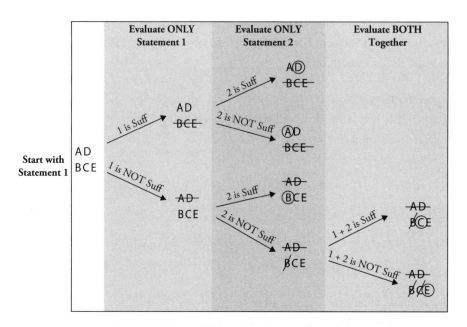

Here is the rephrased problem:

If $xyz \neq 0$, is $z = x$?

(1) $y = 3$ and $x = 2$
(2) $z = -x$

Statement (1) is useless by itself because it says nothing about z. Cross off the top row of answers: $\dfrac{\text{AD}}{\text{BCE}}$

Statement (2) turns out to be very useful. None of the variables is 0, so if $z = -x$, then those two numbers cannot be equal to each other. This statement is sufficient to answer the question: no, z does not equal x. You can circle B on your grid: $\dfrac{\text{AD}}{\text{BCE}}$

The correct answer is (**B**).

If you decide to start with statement (2), your process is almost identical, but you'll use the BD/ACE grid instead. For example:

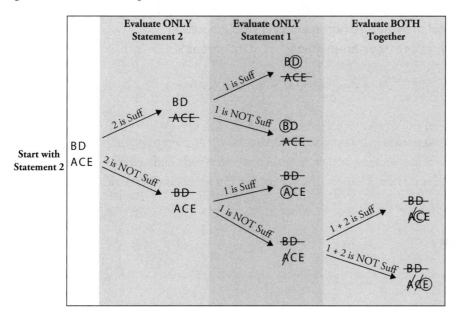

First, evaluate statement (1) by itself and, if you've crossed off answers (A), (B), and (D), then evaluate the two statements together.

Whether you use AD/BCE or BD/ACE, remember to

- cross off the *top* row if the first statement you try is *not* sufficient, and
- cross off the *bottom* row if the first statement you try *is* sufficient.

Pop Quiz! Test Your Skills

Have you learned the DS process? If not, go back through the chapter and work through the sample problems again. Try writing out each step yourself.

If so, prove it! Give yourself up to four minutes total to try the following two problems:

1. Are there more engineers than salespeople working at SoHo Corp?

    (1) SoHo Corp employs $\frac{2}{3}$ as many clerical staff as engineers and salespeople combined.

    (2) If 3 more engineers were employed by SoHo Corp and the number of salespeople remained the same, then the number of engineers would be double the number of salespeople employed by the company.

2. At SoHo Corp, what is the ratio of managers to non-managers?

   (1) If there were 3 more managers and the number of salespeople remained the same, then the ratio of managers to non-managers would double.
   (2) There are 4 times as many non-managers as managers at SoHo Corp.

How did it go? Are you very confident in your answers? Somewhat confident? Not at all confident?

Before you check your answers, go back over your work, using the DS process discussed in this chapter as your guide. Where can you improve? Did you write down (and use!) your answer grid? Did you look at each statement separately before looking at them together (if necessary)? Did you mix up any of the steps of the process? How neat is the work on your scrap paper? You may want to rewrite your work before you review the answers.

Pop Quiz Answer Key

1. Engineers vs. Salespeople

Step 1: Is this a Value or Yes/No question?

   1. Are there more engineers than salespeople working at SoHo Corp?

This is a Yes/No question.

Steps 2 and 3: What is given and what is the question? Rephrase the question.

The question stem doesn't contain any given information. In this case, the question is already about as simplified as it can get: are there more engineers than salespeople?

Step 4: Evaluate the statements.

If you start with the first statement, use the AD/BCE answer grid.

   (1) SoHo Corp employs $\frac{2}{3}$ as many clerical staff as engineers and salespeople combined.

If you add up the engineers and salespeople, then there are fewer people on the clerical staff…but this indicates nothing about the relative number of engineers and salespeople. This statement is not sufficient. Cross off (A) and (D), the top row, of your answer grid.

   (2) If 3 more engineers were employed by SoHo Corp and the number of salespeople remained the same, then the number of engineers would be double the number of salespeople employed by the company.

This one sounds promising. If you add only 3 engineers, then you'll have twice as many engineers as salespeople. Surely, that means there are more engineers than salespeople?

Don't jump to any conclusions. Test some possible numbers; think about fairly extreme scenarios. What if you start with just 1 engineer? When you add 3, you'll have 4 engineers. If there are 4 engineers, then there are half as many, or 2, salespeople. In other words, you start with 1 engineer and 2 salespeople, so there are more salespeople. Interesting.

According to this one case, the answer to the Yes/No question *Are there more engineers than salespeople?* is no.

Can you find a yes answer? Try a larger set of numbers. If you start with 11 engineers and add 3, then you would have 14 total. The number of salespeople would have to be 7. In this case, then, there are more engineers to start than salespeople, so the answer to the question *Are there more engineers than salespeople?* is yes.

Because you can find both yes and no answers, statement (2) is not sufficient. Cross off answer (B).

Now, try the two statements together. How does the information about the clerical staff combine with statement (2)?

Whenever you're trying some numbers and you have to examine the two statements together, see whether you can reuse the numbers that you tried earlier.

If you start with 1 engineer, you'll have 2 salespeople, for a total of 3. In this case, you'd have 2 clerical staff, and the answer to the original question is no.

If you start with 11 engineers, you'll have 7 salespeople, for a total of 18. In this case, you'd have 12 clerical staff, and the answer to the original question is yes.

The correct answer is **(E)**. The information is not sufficient even when both statements are used together.

2. Managers vs. Non-Managers

Step 1: Is this a Value or a Yes/No question?

      2. At SoHo Corp, what is the ratio of managers to non-managers?

This is a Value question. You need to find one specific ratio—or know that you can find one specific ratio—in order to answer the question.

Steps 2 and 3: What is given and what is the question? Rephrase the question.

Find the ratio of managers to non-managers, or $M:N$.

Step 4: Evaluate the statements.

If you start with the second statement, use the BD/ACE answer grid. (Note: this is always your choice; the solution with the BD/ACE grid shown is just for practice.)

> (2) There are 4 times as many non-managers as managers at SoHo Corp.

If there is 1 manager, there are 4 non-managers. If there are 2 managers, there are 8 non-managers. If there are 3 managers, there are 12 non-managers.

What does that mean? In each case, the ratio of managers to non-managers is the same, $1:4$. Even though you don't know how many managers and non-managers there are, you do know the ratio. (For more on ratios, see the Ratios chapter of this book.

This statement is sufficient; cross (A), (C), and (E), the bottom row, off of the grid.

> (1) If there were 3 more managers and the number of salespeople remained the same,
>   then the ratio of managers to non-managers would double.

First, what does it mean to *double* a ratio? If the starting ratio were $2:3$, then doubling that ratio would give you $4:3$. The first number in the ratio doubles relative to the second number.

Test some cases. If you start with 1 manager, then 3 more would bring the total number of managers to 4. The *manager* part of the ratio just quadrupled (1 to 4), not doubled, so this number is not a valid starting point. Discard this case.

If you have to add 3 and want that number to double, then you need to start with 3 managers. When you add 3 more, that portion of the ratio doubles from 3 to 6. The other portion, the non-managers, remains the same.

Notice anything? The statement says nothing about the relative number of non-managers. The starting ratio could be $3:2$ or $3:4$ or $3:14$, for all you know. In each case, doubling the number of managers would double the ratio (to $6:2$, or $6:4$, or $6:14$). You can't figure out the specific ratio from this statement.

The correct answer is **(B)**: statement (2) is sufficient, but statement (1) is not.

Proving Insufficiency

The Pop Quiz solutions used the Testing Cases strategy: testing real numbers to help determine whether a statement is sufficient. You can do this whenever the problem allows for the possibility of multiple numbers or cases.

When you're doing this, your goal is to try to prove the statement insufficient. For example:

> If x and y are positive integers, is the sum of x and y between 20 and 26, inclusive?
>
> (1) $x - y = 6$

Test your first case. You're allowed to pick any numbers for x and y that make statement 1 true *and* that follow any constraints given in the question stem. In this case, that means the two numbers have to be positive integers and that $x - y$ has to equal 6.

Case #1: $20 - 14 = 6$. These numbers make statement 1 true and follow the constraint in the question stem, so these are legal numbers to pick. Now, try to answer the Yes/No question: $20 + 14 = 34$, so no, the sum is not between 20 and 26, inclusive.

You now have a *no* answer. Can you think of another set of numbers that will give you the opposite, a *yes* answer?

Case #2: $15 - 9 = 6$. In this case, the sum is 24, so the answer to the Yes/No question is yes, the sum is between 20 and 26, inclusive.

Because you have found both a yes and a no answer, the statement is not sufficient.

Here's a summary of the process:

1. Notice that you can test cases. You can do this when the problem allows for multiple possible values.

2. Pick numbers that make the statement true and that follow any givens in the question stem. If you realize that you picked numbers that make the statement false or contradict givens in the question stem, *discard* those numbers and start over.

3. Your first case will give you one answer: a yes or a no on a Yes/No problem, or a numerical value on a value problem.

4. Try to find a second case that gives you a *different* answer. On a Yes/No problem, you'll be looking for the opposite of what you found for the first case. For a Value problem, you'll be looking for a different numerical answer. (Don't forget that whatever you pick still has to make the statement true and follow the givens in the question stem!)

The usefulness of trying to prove insufficiency is revealed as soon as you find two different answers. You're done! That statement is not sufficient, so you can cross off an answer or answers and move to the next step.

What if you keep finding the same answer? Try this:

> If *x* and *y* are positive integers, is the product of *x* and *y* between 20 and 26, inclusive?
>
> (1) *x* is a multiple of 17.

Case #1: Test $x = 17$. Since *y* must be a positive integer, try the smallest possible value first: $y = 1$. In this case, the product is 17, which is not between 20 and 26 inclusive. The answer to the question is *no*; can you find the opposite answer?

Case #2: If you make $x = 34$, then *xy* will be too big, so keep $x = 17$. The next smallest possible value for *y* is 2. In this case, the product is 34, which is also not between 20 and 26 inclusive. The answer is again no.

Can you think of a case where you will get a *yes* answer? No! The smallest possible product is 17, and the next smallest possible product is 34. Any additional values of *x* and *y* you try will be equal to or larger than 34.

You've just proved the statement sufficient because it is impossible to find a yes answer. Testing Cases can help you to figure out the "theory" answer, or the mathematical reasoning that proves the statement is sufficient.

This won't always work so cleanly. Sometimes, you'll keep getting all no answers or all yes answers but you won't be able to figure out the theory behind it all. If you test three or four different cases, and you're actively seeking out the opposite answer but never find it, then go ahead and assume that the statement is sufficient, even if you're not completely sure why.

Do make sure that you're trying numbers with different characteristics. Try both even and odd. Try a prime number. Try zero or a negative or a fraction. (You can only try numbers that are allowed by the problem, of course. In the case of the above problems, you were only allowed to try positive integers.)

Here's how Testing Cases would work on a Value problem:

> If *x* and *y* are prime numbers, what is the product of *x* and *y*?
>
> (1) The product is even.

Case #1: $x = 2$ and $y = 3$. Both numbers are prime numbers and their product is even, so these are legal numbers to try. In this case, the product is 6. Can you choose numbers that will give a different product?

Case #2: $x = 2$ and $y = 5$. Both numbers are prime numbers and their product is even, so these are legal numbers to try. In this case, the product is 10.

The statement is not sufficient because there are at least two different values for the product of x and y.

In short, when you're evaluating DS statements, go into them with an "I'm going to try to prove you insufficient!" mindset.

- If you do find two different answers (yes and no, or two different numbers), then immediately declare that statement not sufficient.

- If, after several tries, you keep finding the same answer despite trying different kinds of numbers, see whether you can articulate why; that statement may be sufficient after all. Even if you can't say why, go ahead and assume that the statement is sufficient.

Now you're ready to test your Data Sufficiency skills. As you work through the chapters in this book, test your progress using some of the *Official Guide* problem set lists found online, in your Manhattan Prep Student Center. Start with lower-numbered problems first, in order to practice the process, and work your way up to more and more difficult problems.

GO BEYOND BOOKS.
TRY A FREE CLASS NOW.

IN-PERSON COURSE

ONLINE COURSE

GMAT® INTERACT™

Find a GMAT course near you and attend the first session free, no strings attached. You'll meet your instructor, learn how the GMAT is scored, review strategies for Data Sufficiency, dive into Sentence Correction, and gain insights into a wide array of GMAT principles and strategies.

Enjoy the flexibility of prepping from home or the office with our online course. Your instructor will cover all the same content and strategies as an in-person course, while giving you the freedom to prep where you want. Attend the first session free to check out our cutting-edge online classroom.

GMAT Interact is a comprehensive self-study program that is fun, intuitive, and driven by you. Each interactive video lesson is taught by an expert instructor and can be accessed on your computer or mobile device. Lessons are personalized for you based on the choices you make.

Find your city at
manhattanprep.com/gmat/classes

See the full schedule at
manhattanprep.com/gmat/classes

Try 5 full lessons for free at
manhattanprep.com/gmat/interact

Not sure which is right for you? Try all three!
Or give us a call and we'll help you figure out
which program fits you best.

Toll-Free U.S. Number (800) 576-4628 | **International** 001 (212) 721-7400 | **Email** gmat@manhattanprep.com

PREP MADE PERSONAL

Whether you want quick coaching in a particular GMAT subject area or a comprehensive study plan developed around your goals, we've got you covered. Our expert, 99th percentile GMAT tutors can help you hit your top score.

CHECK OUT THESE REVIEWS FROM MANHATTAN PREP TUTORING STUDENTS.

CALL OR EMAIL US AT **800-576-4628** OR **GMAT@MANHATTANPREP.COM**
FOR INFORMATION ON RATES AND TO GET PAIRED WITH YOUR GMAT TUTOR.